ISAAC NEWTON
Mastermind of Modern Science

Newton with his prism and silent face
. . . a mind forever
Voyaging through strange seas of thought, alone.
                    —WILLIAM WORDSWORTH

Newton and his reflecting telescope.

A FIRST BIOGRAPHY

ISAAC NEWTON

Mastermind of Modern Science

by David C. Knight

Pictures by John Griffin

FRANKLIN WATTS, INC.

575 Lexington Avenue, New York 22

FIRST PRINTING

Library of Congress Catalog Card Number 61–5278

Copyright © 1961 by Franklin Watts, Inc.

MANUFACTURED IN THE UNITED STATES OF AMERICA

Contents

[v]

CONTENTS

ISAAC NEWTON
Mastermind of Modern Science

————◆————

ONE

The Mastermind

————◆ • ◆————

IN A SMALL Lincolnshire manor house at Woolsthorpe, England, on Christmas Day, 1642, a child was born who—so said his mother—was so small that he could have fitted into a quart jug. For many weeks, he was so frail that his little head had to be supported by a kind of scarf about his neck.

Yet within that tiny head a great mind was to develop—a mind whose thoughts and ideas were to influence the world of science for centuries afterward.

When, from time to time in history, such a truly gifted mind comes forth, it can be called, in every sense of the word, a *mastermind.*

It also happened that in the same year, the world lost another scientific mastermind—Galileo Galilei. History, as if to make up for that loss, gave the world the frail baby of Woolsthorpe.

As in the case of Galileo, this baby did not come from a particularly brilliant family. His father followed the calling of most of his ancestors, who had been little else than common farmers tilling the quiet Lincolnshire countryside. Nor could the baby's mother boast of anyone on her side of the family who had been outstanding in any way.

The baby's father had died three months before his birth, and later the widowed mother remarried. Still, when children came again to her, they were in no way as gifted as the child born to her on Christmas Day in 1642.

This child, whose fragile head contained one of the greatest minds the world has ever known, lived to be eighty-five. His name was Isaac Newton.

TWO

Early Years
in Lincolnshire

Young Isaac Newton lived for many years in the manor house at Woolsthorpe. It was nestled in a fertile rolling valley just a few minutes walk from the Parish Church of Colsterworth where Isaac was baptized on January 1, 1643.

The Lincolnshire youth's upbringing was left largely to his maternal grandmother, Mrs. Ayscough, of whom Isaac was especially fond. When Isaac's father died, shortly before the birth of his famous son, friends and relatives urged the Widow Newton to marry again.

Hannah Newton, then about thirty-five years of age, finally accepted the proposal of a kind and elderly clergyman named Barnabas Smith, who lived in the nearby village of North Witham. Here she moved to begin a new life with her second husband, and to bear him a son and two daughters.

Although Hannah was sad to leave Isaac in her mother's care, she was also grateful to Reverend Smith for giving Isaac a small portion of land in nearby Sewstern. With this to fall back on, at least the lad would never go hungry.

Hannah knew, too, that by cart it was but a short ride of a mile to Woolsthorpe. She visited Isaac and her mother often, knowing that her brother George would take care of the farm safely until Isaac became old enough to run it himself.

Newton's birthplace, the Manor House at Woolsthorpe. (After a contemporary drawing.)

Isaac attended small, one-room country schools at Stoke and Skillington until he was eleven. He was also fortunate to be under the watchful eye of the Reverend William Ayscough, Hannah Smith's older brother and Isaac's uncle. Ayscough encouraged the country lad in his studies, perhaps observing in Isaac's nimble hands and quiet thoughtfulness something more than just another farmer-to-be.

Little is really known of Isaac's life during these quiet years at Woolsthorpe. Doubtless he spent many happy summer days beside the tiny river Witham, which wandered slowly northward to Grantham and beyond. Round about him were many things to watch and observe—the darting field mice and gaily colored birds, the swift fish in the stream and the tall, waving grass that grew beside it. There were chores to be done, too, and Isaac must have helped George Ayscough many times in shoeing the large dray horses, salting meat for the winter, plowing the fertile land, and shearing the woolly Lincolnshire sheep.

Yet not all of these days could have been quiet ones, for England at this time was in a period of violent change. Many people moaned that it was a bad time to be alive—the nights could be filled with sudden terror.

For Isaac was growing up in the midst of Cromwellian England. In 1649, the king, Charles I, had been put to death by his angry subjects and now England was ruled by a military Commonwealth headed by Oliver Cromwell, who called himself "Lord High Protector." Actually, Cromwell had all the powers of a dictator.

Day and night Cromwell's troops scoured the English countryside in search of "malignants" as he called them—followers of the royal family who had gone into hiding. These royalists were also known as Cavaliers because they wore their hair in long curls, while Cromwell's men who hunted them were called Roundheads because of their closely-cropped heads.

Isaac must have seen soldiers of both sides galloping about the country roads of Colsterworth, engaging in raids and counterraids. Perhaps the manor house itself at Woolsthorpe was even searched by arrogant Roundheads in

A clash between the Roundheads and the Cavaliers near Colsterworth.

search of Cavaliers. Colsterworth was the home of many Cromwell sympathizers, and Isaac might even have seen the smoke of a distant barn burned by Cavaliers who came out of hiding from time to time to annoy their enemies.

Under this shadow of civil war, Isaac reached the age of

twelve when, largely at the insistence of the Reverend Ayscough, he was sent to the Kings School at Grantham to continue his education.

In the countryside where Isaac was growing up, Grantham was the nearest town of any size. It had some three thousand inhabitants.

But Grantham was also seven miles away from Woolsthorpe. Reverend Ayscough and Isaac's mother, Hannah Smith, on one of their meetings at Woolsthorpe, discussed the problem of Isaac's getting to Grantham and back each day. It was finally decided that the daily journey of fourteen miles would be too far and that Isaac would have to live in Grantham itself.

"But with whom can he lodge there?" asked Reverend Ayscough.

"I know just the person," said Isaac's mother. "Mrs. Clark on High Street. We were friends as children, and she is now married to an apothecary. Perhaps they could give Isaac board and lodging."

So it was that Isaac Newton went to live with the lively Clark family in their house next to the George Inn at Grantham.

Isaac found much there to interest him. In Mr. Clark's apothecary shop, for example, there were the many-colored chemicals and medicines in all sorts of bottles and vials. Probably it was here that Isaac's lifelong love of chemistry was born.

There was also pretty and clever Anne Storey, who was Mrs. Clark's daughter by her first marriage. Anne was about Isaac's age and the two became friends. Isaac used his talented hands often to make and repair toy furniture for Anne. Mr. Clark, who was very kind to Isaac, encouraged him to make things with his hands, in addition to allowing him to help in the apothecary shop.

Isaac Newton in Mr. Clark's apothecary shop at Grantham.

While he was living with the Clarks, Isaac discovered a book called *The Mysteries of Air and Nature*. From it he learned to put together things like simple fireworks, machines, and equipment for doing tricks. In it too were hints on how to draw, paint, and perform other handicrafts. Soon Isaac was keeping his own notebook, copying out suggestions for drawing and making colors for painting.

Young Newton seemed to have a passion for making things of all sorts. He chiseled out a workable sundial on a stone of his house (still preserved by the Royal Society of England today). He made an exact working model of a windmill, which he saw some men building on the nearby Gunnerby Road. He could make anything from a wheeled chair to a water clock. Isaac also made many kites, attaching lanterns to their tails and flying them at night to the fright of neighboring peasants, who thought they were comets.

Isaac seemed to show no signs of his developing mastermind at this time. A person seeing him would have said that he was a normal, mechanically talented boy in his early teens.

Meanwhile, however, Isaac was doing poorly at his schoolwork. In fact, the boy from Lincolnshire cared so little for his studies that he stood at the bottom of the lowest *form,* or class, at the Kings School.

Aside from his poor showing at school, Isaac seemed merely an ordinary boy, not especially strong, inclined to be silent and dreamy. Newton himself later wrote that he had very little in common with his schoolmates and seldom joined in their games.

Odd though it may seem, it is entirely possible that a savage kick in the stomach caused the great Newton's mind to awaken.

An older boy at the Kings School took a dislike to the quiet, dreamy Isaac. Often this boy would laugh at and make fun of Newton. One afternoon the older student went farther than usual: he gave Newton a painful kick in the stomach.

Isaac flew into a rage at the insult and tore into the bully, giving the older boy such a pounding with his fists that his tormentor tumbled to the ground.

Meanwhile a crowd had gathered to watch the fight. Among them was young Stokes, also a student and the son of the school's headmaster.

Stokes began to cheer Newton on. He had often seen the bully beating smaller boys at the school.

Soon all the fight had gone out of the older boy.

"He's a coward, Newton," yelled Stokes. "Rub his face in the dirt!"

Isaac did so. Soon the beaten bully slunk away, never to bother Isaac again.

This incident had a far more valuable effect on Newton than merely giving him the satisfaction of beating a bully. The other boy had stood far above him in his schoolwork. Then and there Isaac determined to surpass him in his studies as well.

Stung into activity, he really began to work hard on every subject in the school curriculum. Headmaster Stokes was surprised and delighted with his scholar's progress. For the first time in his life Newton was showing how fine a mind he had. He had been idle at school only because other things had interested him more deeply. Soon his single-minded effort carried him to the proud position of top boy at Kings School.

In 1656, when Isaac was fourteen, his stepfather, the Reverend Barnabas Smith, died. Hannah Smith, seeing no reason to stay on at North Witham, returned to the manor house at Woolsthorpe. With her she brought Isaac's half brother and sisters—Benjamin, Mary, and Hannah Smith. Isaac became good friends with these children. All through his life he was to help them, and later he was to make them his heirs.

Isaac's mother was now in the position of needing a man to take charge of the family estate and to farm the land. What was more natural than to call Isaac home and give him this responsibility—especially since he was the lawful heir to Woolsthorpe?

Hannah Smith did not reach this decision overnight, however. Previously she and Reverend Ayscough had wanted to let Isaac finish at the Kings School. But Hannah, now a widow for the second time, was finding it harder and harder to make ends meet. Cromwell's suspicious troops were everywhere. Taxes were higher. Innocent people were being deported from England. Neighbor began to distrust neighbor. Wages had risen sharply, while trade dipped dangerously. Hired help was hard to find.

Reluctantly, Isaac Newton said good-by to the Clark family at Grantham and returned to Woolsthorpe.

As a farmer, young Newton proved to be a dismal failure. No doubt if he had been interested in agricultural matters, he might have made a success of it. But the fact was that he was not the least bit interested. He hungered for mechanical things to experiment with and books to study.

The well-known story of young Newton's strange behavior during a storm illustrates how poorly suited he was to farm routine.

This violent storm occurred in September of 1658, just a few days before the death of Oliver Cromwell—almost as if to mark that event. Hannah Smith, fearing that the wild fury of the gale would surely tear the barn doors loose if they were not securely latched, sent Isaac out to shut them. Half an hour passed and the lad did not return.

Wondering what could be delaying Isaac, Hannah wrapped her shawl tightly about her shoulders and made her way to the barn.

The first thing she saw was the barn door, ripped from its hinges and lying on the ground. Moreover, inside the barn she discovered her son, playing a game!

"Whatever are you doing, lad?" she asked.

Isaac looked at her dreamily. He had been jumping repeatedly from the window ledge to the ground, first this way, then that, marking the spot where he fell each time.

"I am measuring the force of the wind, Mother. See? When the gusts are very strong, my jumps are longer."

It did not take many more such incidents for Hannah Smith to realize that Isaac was simply not suited to a farmer's life.

There are other stories, too, of Newton's growing absent-mindedness. Once an idea had occurred to him, he could think of nothing else, no matter what went on about him.

Once when Isaac was leading a horse down the road, the horse slipped out of its bridle and trotted back to its stable alone. Newton, however, thinking deeply of some idea or other, continued walking with the bridle in his hand, unaware that the horse was no longer with him.

On another occasion he dismounted to lead his horse up a particularly steep hill. When they reached the top, Isaac forgot to remount, and led the horse the rest of the way home on foot.

After two years of trying, Hannah Smith finally realized that she had better forget about making a farmer out of the boy. Isaac would rather read, or make things with his hands, write in his notebook, or just plain daydream. Hannah discussed the problem of Isaac with her brother.

As usual, the Reverend Ayscough saw the matter clearly. Isaac was different from the raw country lads with whom he had gone to school at Stoke and Skillington. He had a great deal of the scholar about him. Still keenly interested in Isaac's future, Reverend Ayscough urged Hannah Smith to allow the boy to continue his education at the Kings School.

"And—" declared the Reverend, after his sister had nodded her head in agreement, "when Isaac has finished his studies at Grantham, he must go on to the University at Cambridge."

It took time for Hannah Smith to get used to the idea, but secretly she was pleased. Her Isaac—to become a university scholar—and a gentleman! But there was the expense to think about; she was not a wealthy woman by any means. Yet perhaps she would find a way when the time came.

Accordingly, in the fall of 1660, Isaac once more returned to the Clark house on High Street. Anne Storey, of course, was delighted to see him again. Between the two young people an early love may have developed; it is possible that they discussed marriage sometime in the future. But for the time being, Isaac had his studies to think about.

Until his graduation from the Kings School in 1661, Newton worked hard for his goal—Cambridge. His reputation as a fine student grew quickly. When graduation day finally arrived, both Hannah Smith and Reverend Ayscough heard Headmaster Stokes say this about Isaac:

"The student of which Kings School is most proud in this class is . . . Master Isaac Newton."

No one could have been more grateful than young Newton for the headmaster's words. But he was glad for another reason, too.

He knew that his application for entrance into Cambridge University had just been accepted.

THREE

Newton Goes to Cambridge

———◆◆◆———

I N 1661, at the age of eighteen, Isaac Newton began his studies at Cambridge University. He had been enrolled at the famous Trinity College—the same college that his uncle, Reverend Ayscough, had attended.

The fifty-mile trip from Woolsthorpe to Cambridge had been a long, hard one for Isaac. Because the roads were poor and there were vicious highwaymen about, the trip by coach had taken all of two days. Isaac was exhausted. Shy and alone in his new surroundings, it took him several days to recover from the trip.

Reverend Ayscough had given Isaac a letter of introduction to Mr. Pulleyne, a Fellow of Trinity College, and the young student from Woolsthorpe was enrolled under his charge.

Because Isaac's mother was not a rich woman, she had been unable to provide her son with much money. Thus Isaac joined the College as a "sizar"—a student who paid his way during his stay there by waiting on his tutor and doing all sorts of odd jobs not required of wealthier students.

Besides being a poor country boy with no important acquaintances, Newton was studious and shy by nature. He spent little time with his fellow-students at Trinity. Many of these were loose-living sons of either noblemen or well-to-do parents, and they were not interested in the quiet, bookish young man from Lincolnshire.

There was, however, one student at Trinity who became Isaac's friend. His name was John Wickens and the two young men soon discovered that they had many things in common. Both were quiet, studious, and determined to educate themselves.

At this time Cambridge was greatly overcrowded and often three and sometimes four students were assigned to the same quarters. Newton and Wickens had both been unfortunate in drawing roommates of wild and rowdy natures. Just as the two had settled down to their books, in would burst these wealthy young men, who almost always wanted to drink, gamble, and make a lot of noise.

One night, when they had finally given up trying to study and had escaped to the quiet of Trinity's Great Court, Newton and Wickens met.

They walked in silence for some minutes and then Wickens, brightening, turned to Isaac.

"I say, Newton, wouldn't it be fine if we could share quarters? Perhaps we could persuade our present roommates to move in with each other."

The young men decided to appeal to the College authorities and, in a short time, their request was granted. Newton joyfully moved in with his friend, and the two continued to share quarters for many years.

As a young student at Trinity College, Newton was surrounded by the vast store of valuable books and manuscripts in the library; he heard lectures on Greek, Latin, mathematics, and theology. His mind started to awaken. He began to show his brilliance. More than once his tutors remarked to each other about his progress. They soon found that the serious young student from Lincolnshire often showed uncanny knowledge of subjects that were to form the topics of *future* lectures. Isaac, on his own, had mastered them independently and purely because he was interested.

The result was that he was soon excused from attending certain courses. This left him free to search out any pieces of knowledge that struck his fancy. And there were many.

Isaac's chief interests seemed to center more and more on physics and mathematics. Johannes Kepler's *Optics* was one of the first books he read at Trinity. Newton was to make some of his first discoveries in the field of *optics*—the science of light, what causes it, and what its effects are.

Once, at a fair held in Cambridge, the young man was attracted by a book on astrology. He picked it up and read it. Apparently it contained a number of problems in geometry—a subject of which Isaac was ignorant. Shortly afterward he bought a copy of Euclid's *Elements of Geometry*.

Oddly enough, Newton appeared not to be interested in this book. To his practical mind it seemed that Euclid's geometrical statements were so evident that they did not need proof.

But Isaac was to regret his not having studied Euclid's book more thoroughly. A few years later when he was competing for a scholarship, the examiners warned him about his scanty knowledge of geometry. Isaac won the scholarship anyway, but he was forced to go back and study Euclid more carefully.

When Newton was twenty-one years old, he came under the influence of an older man named Isaac Barrow. Professor Barrow had been recently appointed to the University's famous Lucasian Chair of Mathematics, named after Henry Lucas who had provided the money to endow the professorship.

Barrow was only thirty-three but had already won a reputation as a gifted mathematician, a classical scholar, and a forceful preacher. He was a lively, tough, wiry little man who had attended Trinity some years before, had been made a Fellow of the College in 1649, and later had been driven from England for speaking out against Cromwell. It was said of Barrow that he was afraid of no one.

Barrow soon saw that Isaac Newton showed unusual talent as a scientist—or "natural philosopher" as scientists were called in Newton's time. Barrow befriended and encouraged young Newton. He had been through some exciting adventures during his exile on the European continent, and was a man of the world. Newton, who was to see little of the world in his whole life, must have listened open-mouthed to the adventurous tales that the forceful Barrow told of his younger days.

The Lucasian Professor was also a specialist in the science of optics, as far as it had been developed at that time. It was while working under Barrow that Newton began grinding his first lenses—curved pieces of glass—for making experiments with light.

Barrow was astonished at the young man's quick prog-

When Isaac Newton was twenty-one, he came under the influence of Professor Isaac Barrow.

ress. Later, in 1699, when Barrow was to publish his lectures on optics, he turned to his brilliant student for help. It was also Barrow who saw that Newton had a genius for mathematics, and urged him really to study Euclid's geometry.

Isaac's mind was also busy with *refraction,* or the bending of light. He was experimenting with his lenses and thinking about the things Professor Barrow told him. From his school days on, Isaac had been an experimenter, who liked to put his thoughts to proof. He wanted particularly to understand the events that took place naturally in the world around him—motions of planets and comets, the changing of the tides, the beautiful colors in soap bubbles, the resistance of the air, the laws of motion, and the transmuting or changing of one metal into another.

Things in nature behaved either in certain ways, or they didn't, Isaac decided. If one thing didn't work, perhaps another would. Supplied with books and scientific equipment at Trinity, Newton began experimenting in earnest. And for relaxation, he always turned to *alchemy*—the recombining of one natural substance into another—which, while it was not a science, was the forerunner of modern chemistry.

Cambridge at this time was not considered the most advanced center of English mathematics. Scientists—or "natural philosophers"—felt that more progress was being made by scholars in London and at Oxford. In a short time, however, the quiet student from Woolsthorpe was to bring the highest mathematical honor to his own university.

Early in the year 1665, just a few months before he was to take his Bachelor of Arts degree, Isaac worked out a basic formula, or rule, which has been used ever since in mathematics. Today we call it the *binomial theorem*. A *binomial* is any two numbers connected by the plus (+) sign or minus (—) sign. *7 + 4* and *3,567,438 — 1,999,563* are both binomials. A *theorem* is a formula or rule.

Sometimes, in figuring scientific or mathematical problems, binomials have to be multiplied by themselves many, many times. Multiplications like this—of which Newton had to do many—are very complicated. They could cover sheets and sheets of paper were it not for Isaac Newton's rule, the *binomial theorem*, which looks like this:

$$(X + Y)^n = X^n + NX^{n-1}Y + \frac{n(n-1)}{1 \cdot 2}X^{n-2}Y^2$$
$$+ \frac{n(n-1)(n-2)}{1 \cdot 2 \cdot 3}X^{n-3}Y^3 + \cdots$$

It looks difficult, but scientists with an understanding of mathematics substitute the numbers they have for the letters, and follow the multiplication signs and the plus and minus signs in the formula. By so doing, they can get correct answers to their problems simply and quickly—without covering all those sheets of paper.

The *binomial theorem* works for all numbers (as long as they are in a binomial) and it may be used not just in multiplying a number in itself, but in multiplying *anything*—the number of stars in a galaxy, the number of atoms in a molecule. Moreover, it may be employed to reach answers beyond our understanding, their numbers are so large.

If, in his lifetime, Isaac Newton had gone on to achieve nothing else than the *binomial theorem*, he still would have earned an honored name in scientific history. So important is this theorem that mention of it is engraved on his tombstone. But at the time he stated it, he was barely twenty-two years old!

Newton's genius was indeed developing.

And so was Isaac as a person. He was becoming less shy, more sure of himself. Just knowing Professor Barrow stimulated and encouraged him. He led an ordinary student's life. He visited the local taverns with his schoolfellows. He is even said to have done a bit of gambling—and lost. On vacations he journeyed home to Woolsthorpe, bringing with him small presents for his stepbrother and stepsisters —presents he could ill afford.

The day came at last, early in 1665, when Isaac together with twenty-five others received his Bachelor of Arts degree from Trinity College. The standings of the graduates are not known. Was Newton at the head of his class? Did he distinguish himself in his examination? There is no way of knowing. Later he was to be elected a member of the College, but that was still a few years in coming.

Even as he was standing with the other graduates at graduation ceremonies, Isaac's mind was probably busy with the *binomial theorem*. Also for the last few months his thoughts about light and color had led him to experiment with a prism.

The mastermind was now occupied with many things. Yet it was characteristic of Newton to keep them all to himself. Only a few handwritten notes remain to tell of his thinking at this time. Throughout his whole life, Newton disliked to make public any unfinished project or discovery.

By the time those about him began to suspect that Isaac Newton was doing things of value, he was well on his way to becoming the original thinker we recognize today.

FOUR

The World of Science Before Newton

EVERY great man owes something to the times he lives in and to other men who have worked in his field before him. Isaac Newton was no exception. He did not stand alone as the only discoverer of important laws of nature.

Other great men in England and in Europe were also gaining important scientific knowledge. Newton inherited much from these men, as well as others who had lived before him. "If I have seen further than most men," wrote Newton in his old age, "it is by standing on the shoulders of giants."

When Isaac was growing into young manhood, a whole new awareness of science was coming about in Europe. The experimental method—finding out about things by watching how they behaved—was becoming popular everywhere. More and more scientific publications were being read in France, Italy, and England.

While Isaac was still at the Kings School, the great Royal Society for the Advancement of Learning was founded. Its influence quickly became important throughout all Europe. Educated men everywhere were eager to find out more about science. Even the King of England, Charles II, did chemical experiments in his spare time.

But this new awareness of science had come only gradually. Even while Newton was making his great discoveries, men who called themselves educated still believed what the ancient Greeks had to say about science. The greatest of these was Aristotle and it was to his writings that thinkers turned for the answers to their scientific questions. Whether these questions concerned the movement of the heavenly bodies, or of moving bodies on the earth, Aristotle's word was the final one, just as Euclid's was in matters of geometry. In fact, many learned men in Newton's own day considered that knowledge had gone *downhill* since the time of the Greeks!

The Greek way was not to make experiments to gain knowledge. The real way to find out if a thing was true or not was to think hard about it—then to discuss it with other learned men. Measuring a thing, watching it fall, timing it—these were not the ways by which a true Greek philosopher found out about scientific laws. The Greeks had believed that it was by pure thought—and by pure thought alone, reasoned out according to strictly laid-down principles—that one found out about nature.

In addition, the Greek way was to seek for the "why" of things, not the "how." This was the exact opposite of Isaac Newton's way of studying nature. To him, an ounce of experimental proof was always worth more than a pound of arguing *why* something *might possibly* happen. It was always to be the *how* of things that interested Newton, not the *why*.

In the centuries before Christ, men believed that the earth they lived on was something like a giant pie-tin with the sky as a sort of gigantic cover. Through holes in this cover, the gods let down the stars to make the world more beautiful and to show that they were pleased.

Gradually however, early thinkers came to believe in a spherical, or globelike, earth. The heavenly bodies, including the sun, the moon, and the twinkling points of light called stars, were seen to have certain movements. Although their paths varied during the year, the sun and moon moved westward across the sky each day. With few exceptions, so did the stars, although the rising and setting of any one of them varied from night to night.

The early astronomers came to believe that the heavens as a whole revolved about the earth. The sun took a year to go around the earth and the moon a month.

The trouble was, however, that as men continued to study the heavens, they saw that certain stars went against this theory. These stars were named *planets,* or "wanderers." They seemed to move without regard to the movement of other stars. When the stars moved in one direction, the planets might suddenly start moving directly *opposite!*

In the second century A.D. in Alexandria, Egypt, there lived a great Greek scientist named Claudius Ptolemaeus, who is generally known as Ptolemy. He wrote a book called the *Almagest,* which in Arabic means "Great System." In this book Ptolemy gathered together all the earlier astronomical ideas of the Greeks, but also added many of his own. Ptolemy's scheme of the solar system came to be known by his name—the *Ptolemaic System.*

Ptolemy taught that the earth was the fixed center of the whole universe, around which all the other heavenly bodies revolved in circles. Ptolemy, however, knew that his system would also have to explain the strange motions of the "wanderers," or planets. Sometimes they moved to the west, sometimes to the east. Ptolemy invented a system of *epicycles* to account for this.

Look at the diagram on the next page and you will understand what epicycles are. They are small circles, whose centers travel along the outsides of much larger circles, called *deferents.* Each planet looped about in an epicycle, at the same time as it revolved about the earth on its deferent. To an observer on earth, this system explained very well why the planets seemed to move back and forth opposite the general motion of the other stars.

As more and more stars and planets were observed, the Ptolemaic System became more and more complicated. In time it was proved to be quite wrong. Ptolemy's idea of the solar system, however, was accepted without question for many hundreds of years.

But as the centuries passed, later astronomers observing the heavens noticed that many times what they saw did not agree with Ptolemaic "facts." Sometimes a planet was not where it should have been at all. The sun, for example, which was thought to be a planet, did not seem to have an orbit whose center was at the earth's center at all.

It was Nicolaus Copernicus, a Polish monk, who upset

the system of Ptolemy. Copernicus, who lived from 1473 to 1543, said that the earth was not the center of the universe at all, but was simply part of the solar system—one

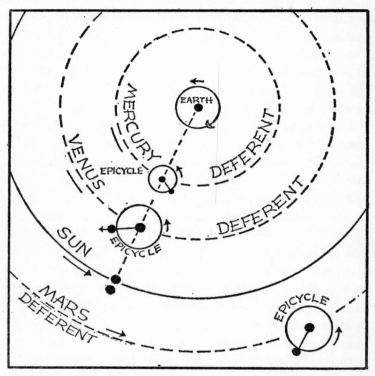

The Ptolemaic System, *showing* epicycles *and* deferents.

of the planets that not only revolved about the sun once each year but spun about on its own axis once every twenty-four hours.

The sun itself, Copernicus said, was the center of the

solar system, and the planets moved around it in regular paths called *orbits*.

The *Copernican System,* like Ptolemy's epicycles, explained many of the heavenly bodies' movements. But it was not fully accepted by church and state authorities until many years after Copernicus' death.

Johannes Kepler, a German mathematician, was the next man to find out important things in astronomy. He did most of his great work at the court of Rudolph II, who was the Holy Roman Emperor. Kepler did much to win the learned men of his day over to the Copernican Theory. Often called the "Lawmaker of the Heavens," he discovered three laws which exactly describe the orbits of the planets and which supported Copernicus' ideas. These laws became the foundation of modern astronomy.

The first of Kepler's laws says that each planet travels in an *ellipse* around the sun, with the sun at one of its *focal points*. An ellipse is a "squashed circle" and always has *two* focal points on its axis, as well as a center point.

The diagram on the next page shows how you can draw an ellipse. Take a length of string and tack both ends of it down to a sheet of paper, leaving the string slack between. Then stretch the string tightly with a pencil whose point is on the paper. Draw the curve above and below the tacks. The curves will connect in a perfect ellipse. The tacks are at the two focal points of the ellipse.

Practically, what Kepler's First Law means is that a planet travels around in an orbit shaped like the ellipse you have just drawn and the sun represents the place where one of your tacks is. Of course, ellipses come in many sizes and shapes. Some are short and some are long, and not every planet's is the same.*

Kepler's famous Second Law of Motion says that the *speed (velocity)* ** of a planet moving around the sun in an

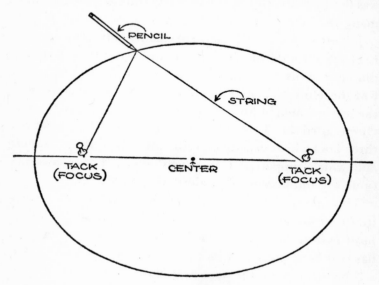

How to draw an ellipse.

ellipse changes all the time. Look at the diagram on the opposite page. It shows that a planet moving around the

---

* As you can see, an ellipse is a curve that closes back on itself. Some curves are curves that are open, such as *parabolas*. Look in the back of this book on page 145 to find out the names of other curves and whether they are open or closed.

** The terms *speed* and *velocity* are often used interchangeably. But more correctly, *speed* measures the rate at which we travel in one direction (a straight line); *velocity* takes into account speed *as well as* direction, as when something moves in a curve.

sun from A to B takes no longer than the same planet moving from C to D. This is so because the area marked 1 is the same as the area marked 2.

Kepler's Third Law says that there is always a definite mathematical relationship between any planet's *distance*

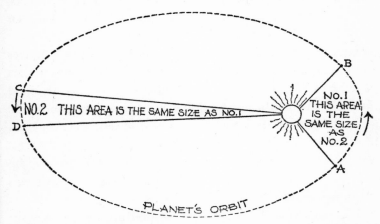

Kepler's famous Second Law, showing that a planet's speed changes as it orbits the sun. The closer the planet gets to the sun the faster it goes. An imaginary line from the planet's center to the sun's center sweeps over equal areas in equal times.

from the sun and the *time* it takes that same planet to orbit the sun. This discovery helps today's scientists locate any given planet in its orbit at any given time.

While Kepler had indeed given the scientific world a valuable set of tools, he failed in correctly explaining them. He had described the motions of the planets, yet what caused them to move as they did?

It was the famous Italian scientist, Galileo Galilei, born

at Pisa in the year of 1564, who was to supply the next important answers to why moving bodies—including the planets—moved as they did. Even though, in his early years, Galileo believed in Ptolemy's ancient system, he later saw that Copernicus was right. And, even though his was far from a complete explanation of moving objects, he was successful in proving many valuable laws of his own by actual experiments.

Galileo was the first to seriously doubt Aristotle's figures on the speed of falling objects. Aristotle had taught that heavier objects fall faster than light ones. Galileo decided to find out for himself by doing his own experiments. He dropped several different objects of different weights from the famous Leaning Tower of Pisa, and saw that they all fell at the same speed—provided their resistance to the air was about the same in each case. In his day, this was an amazing discovery.

Furthermore, Galileo knew that a falling body moved in a special way: the *longer* it fell, the *faster* it continued to fall. This increase in speed, reasoned Galileo, was due to the pull of the earth.

These discoveries led Galileo to suspect a number of things that Isaac Newton was later to prove were absolutely true. Up till the time of Galileo, for example, men thought that whenever an object moved, there was always something called *force* that pushed or pulled it. No force meant no motion.

Galileo was the first to suggest that this was not so. Just because an object moved did not mean there was something called force "pushing" it. Instead he believed that once an object is in motion, it must continue to remain in motion until some *outside force* changes that motion or stops the object altogether. Thus, if a boy rolls a ball along the ground, the ball will eventually stop due to the drag or *friction* with the ground. That is one kind of outside force. Or, if another boy runs up to the ball and gives it a kick while it is still rolling, that would be another kind of outside force.

But, thought Galileo, if that same ball were rolling along in a place where nothing, not even the resistance of the air, could stop it or change its direction, the ball would keep rolling forever. (Outer space, where there is no air-resistance, would be such a place.) Unfortunately, Galileo could not prove this because he could not find or set up the kind of place where an object would move naturally, free of outside forces.

And yet—Galileo had nearly stated Isaac Newton's First Law of Motion!

———◆———

FIVE

Eighteen Months That Changed the World

————◆◆◆————

Iɴ the same year that Isaac Newton graduated from Cambridge, the dreaded bubonic plague broke out in England. Called the "Black Death," it had repeatedly broken out in that country since the fourteenth century. It was carried by ravenous flea-bearing rats, which had again been carelessly allowed to breed and spread their germs in the overcrowded English port cities and towns.

As the great plague swept northward, Cambridge authorities became more and more frightened. London itself had suffered the year before from a mild outbreak of germ-spreading insects, and now fell easy prey to the "Black Death."

Thousands of persons became victims of the terrifying disease. The dead lined the streets in such numbers that not enough healthy men could be found to bury them. In July, August, and September of 1665 the capital city lost nearly a tenth of its population!

Fearing that the pest would surely strike the town of Cambridge and thus endanger the students, the University authorities decided to close down the institution and wait for the great plague to pass. Accordingly, in August, all students were dismissed to their homes. Newton, however, appears to have left for his home at Woolsthorpe a month or two before.

Newton was to spend some eighteen months in "forced exile" at the quiet manor house. Hannah Smith prepared for him a small, almost closetlike room on the second floor. Here Newton began his whole life work. Here he would brood alone on the problems that science had taken as far as it could in 1665. So interested did he become in them that he forgot about the good news Dr. Barrow had brought him before he left Trinity—that a University Fellowship had been talked about for young Newton upon his return. As a Fellow, he would live free at Trinity, be given a small salary for his needs, and have the leisure to study anything he wished.

Being alone at Woolsthorpe in this way had an excellent effect on Newton's gathering genius. He could forget for a time the routine of the University. There were no classes to attend; his mind, stuffed with the latest scientific ideas from Cambridge, could roam at will on any problem it pleased.

England lost thousands to the bubonic plague, yet this dreaded disease provided one of the country's most honored sons with the leisure he needed to think, to inquire, to calculate.

Newton was to spend his twenty-third year, and most of his twenty-fourth, in the quiet of the stone house in

Lincolnshire. His main thinking was to be on three matters—the calculus, gravitation, and optics.

The Calculus

Of this great productive period, Newton was to write
in his old age: "All this was in the two plague years of 1665
and 1666, for in those days I was in the prime of my age for
invention, and minded mathematics and philosophy more
than at any time since."

Mathematics he certainly "minded," for in one of Newton's notebooks there is to be found an account of his first
discovery of "fluxions" in May of 1665. "Fluxions" or
"flowing quantities" was Newton's name for what we now
call *the calculus.*

Without the calculus, modern mathematics would be
greatly hampered. In order to study anything in nature, it
is necessary to deal with quantities that constantly change.
The fact that things are constantly *changing* is one of the
truest statements we can make about them. If we are deal-
ing with the subject of heat, we deal with rates of change
of temperature—cooling off and warming up. An engineer
concerns himself with the rate at which work is being done,
or the position and speed of a moving object.

Very often in the field of mathematics, a mathematician
is faced not only with one thing that is changing, but with
two. To better understand how they are related to one
another, he graphs or *plots* them together, one against the
other, on a set of lines called *coordinates*—two lines drawn
at 90° to each other with their intersecting point at zero.
By using the calculus the mathematician can find out how

his two quantities—whatever they are—are varying with each other at any particular place.

Likewise, in other problems, mathematicians have to deal with the rate of change *of a rate of change*. Often, the *time* changes, too, must be added to a problem. So complicated do these problems sometimes get, it is only by using the calculus that mathematicians and scientists can arrive at an answer.

One of Newton's first problems along these mathematical lines was to figure out part of the space, or *area,* enclosed by an open curve known as a *hyperbola*.

Newton had to use his method of "fluxions" to get his answer. Early in the winter of 1665, he wrote: ". . . I computed the area of the Hyperbola . . . to two and fifty figures . . ." This meant that, to satisfy himself of the most accurate answer, he worked the problem out to fifty-two places to the right of the decimal point. Here the binomial theorem came in handy as well as the "fluxions."

By using mathematical ideas suggested earlier by such men as Cavalieri in Italy, and Kepler in Germany, and developing them further, Isaac began to see how much could be done with the calculus. Indeed, the method of "fluxions" seemed to be the only way that problems involving very tiny quantities could be worked out.

Such quantities—lengths, surfaces, thicknesses, and their rates of growing smaller or larger—were so small that ordinary mathematics could not deal properly with them. And the more Newton worked with them, the more fascinated he became.

Other men might have found these tiny quantities dead

and lifeless things. But to Newton they were every bit as alive as the water that changed from moment to moment in the river Witham. Every bit as alive as the changing seasons at Woolsthorpe!

In discovering this important mathematical method of solving problems, Newton's genius had uncovered something of immense value. And yet, whether he was merely modest or very cautious, he said nothing of it to anyone.

Meanwhile, the great plague continued to take its murderous toll in London, ending in the great fire of 1666. Cambridge remained closed. Not even Newton's closest friends knew of the great ideas taking place in the brain of the young Lincolnshire man.

Universal Gravitation

> Sir Isaac Newton was the boy
>> That climbed the apple tree, sir;
> He then fell down and broke his crown,
>> And lost his gravity, sir.
>>> Sidey, *The Irish Schoolmaster*

While the above verse is amusing, it is not correct, for even if Isaac Newton had fallen from his traditional apple tree he would not have "lost" his gravity.

In fact, this verse contradicts Newton's own Third Law of Motion, which says that for every force exerted there is an equal and opposite reaction. For example, when you press a ball with your finger, the finger is also pressed by the ball.

No force, said Newton, can operate independently from

another. The earth's gravity attracts a falling apple to its surface, but at the same time the apple also pulls the earth upward. However, the upward movement of the earth is extremely small because the earth's size and bulk is so very much greater than the apple's.

Thus Newton would hardly have lost his "gravity" if he had fallen from the apple tree, since at the same time his weight was pressing on the earth, the earth was pressing upward against *him* with an equal and opposite force equal to Newton's own weight.

Whether the story is true or imagined, it is one that is told again and again: In 1666, while Newton was sitting in the manor house garden at Woolsthorpe, he saw an apple fall from a tree.* This triggered certain thoughts that he had been having about gravitation.

Newton had to base his gravitational studies on the facts that were known at the time. But he also had a genius for seeing beyond the facts and getting new meanings from them.

In Newton's mind, the apple became the moon. Like the moon, other large heavenly bodies seemed to move in regular orbits month after month and year after year. What force held them there? The same one that caused the apple to fall to the earth?

On that day in the manor house garden, Newton must have been asking himself many questions:

---

* Due to the popularity of this story, the same tree was so well cared for that it was kept standing until the year 1820 when it was blown down in a storm. From its wood a fine chair was made which can be seen today at Stoke Rochford, England. Oddly enough, later efforts to plant another apple tree in the garden of Woolsthorpe manor house failed completely!

Newton at Woolsthorpe in 1666. Seeing an apple fall triggered certain thoughts he had been having about gravitation.

"Why do the planets go around the sun? Why do they not fly off in straight lines? There must be a greater force pulling them out of their straight-line paths at every moment—clearly this force is the sun's. And what about the moon? It continues to circle the earth and does not fly off in a straight line either. Clearly the force that holds it in a circular path is the earth's. Ah, see there! An apple has fallen from yonder tree. It must be the earth that pulled it down.

"How far up does the earth-force go? No matter how high a mountain we climb, this force seems not to grow less. Could it extend as far as the moon? Could this same force be the force that holds the moon in its path around the earth?

"Indeed," thought Newton, "this is an interesting theory, but how can I hope to prove it? Surely any such proof must contain some law explaining how the gravitational pull of the earth *varies* with the distance from the earth. Clearly it cannot be the same for all distances, even to the ends of the universe. The earth's pull must obviously *grow less* as the distance becomes greater."

For Copernicus and Kepler, as well as for ancient astronomers, the circular motion of the heavenly bodies was considered a "natural motion," just as any material object not held up by something performs the "natural motion" of falling downward.

Isaac Newton was one of the first to question this long-standing idea. Newton's idea—which was the correct one—was that *the only natural motion material objects have is that they move uniformly along a straight line.* Later, this was to become the basis of Newton's First Law of Motion.

For Newton, the fact that the planets orbit the sun, and the moon orbits the earth in *circular motions* (or nearly so; actually they are ellipses that are nearly circles), simply meant that something was interfering with their normal straight-line motion. Some greater force was causing them to go off their straight-line path into the circular paths. They seem to be attracted to some center of force around which their circular motion takes place. Thus, the moon must be revolving around the earth because the earth attracts it. Yet things on the surface of the earth also fall toward it.

Perhaps this was the moment in Newton's thoughts when the apple in the manor house garden fell. For, indeed, the same force that keeps the moon in its monthly orbit around the earth is the same that makes ripe apples fall earthward.

By such thinking, Newton came to consider the motion of the moon around the earth as a *continuous fall* caused by the force of universal gravitation. While the moon always kept about the same distance from the earth, it was continually falling toward it!

Newton knew that two steps had to be taken next. The first was to find out how any gravitational pull would vary with the distance from the body producing that pull. The second was to see whether the earth's pull on the falling apple could also account for the motion of the moon.

That Newton was deeply concerned with these questions at this time is clear, for he wrote ". . . and in the same year (1666) I began to think of gravity extending to the orb of the Moon . . ." By "orb" Newton meant our modern word "orbit."

"How does the pull of the earth's gravity vary with the distance?" Newton kept asking himself.

By doing many calculations, Newton decided that the gravitational pull must *weaken* the farther away an object was from the earth. But by how much? Newton passed many days in figuring. Finally he had the answer! It was his famous *inverse square law*.

An example is the best way to explain this law. The earth, first of all, is a gigantic sphere of matter that causes a powerful gravitational pull on anything near it. This pull, said Newton, is best figured from the *center* of the earth.

If two objects are different distances away from the earth, the earth will exert different pulls on each object. To compare the gravitational pull on each, let us say that one of the objects is 5 times farther from the earth than the other. Then the pull on the farthest object, according to the inverse square law, is only $\frac{1}{25}$ of what it is on the nearer one.

How is this answer arrived at?

We simply take the greater unit-distance away (the number 5) and square it—that is, multiply it by itself—and then make a fraction out of the answer by drawing a line and placing a 1 on top of it—called *inverting* it. Thus, if the farther object were only 3 times as far away as the nearer one, the earth would pull it with a greater force of $\frac{1}{9}$. And if the farther object were as many as 10 times

[45]

as far away as the nearer one, the earth's pull on it would be much weaker, namely $\frac{1}{100}$.

By further reasoning, based on that of Kepler before him, Newton was able to prepare the groundwork for his most important contribution to science: the *law of universal gravitation*. Practically, this law says that large, heavy objects pull each other harder than small, light ones. And the pull is greater between objects near each other than between objects that are far apart. Further, Newton was to suggest that this law operated not only on objects on the earth, but for those in space as well. That was what Newton meant by the word *universal* in his great law—it worked *everywhere* in the universe.

Meditating alone at Woolsthorpe, then, Isaac Newton had succeeded in explaining something that had not occurred to Galileo, Kepler, and others before him. The old question had been: why does not the moon, under the earth's gravitational pull, fall right into the earth as an apple does? Newton's answer was: it *is* falling every moment toward the earth. In a sense, the moon was like a cannon ball—a cannon ball, however, that was falling just as the earth's horizon fell.

The moon fell around the earth; it just followed the earth's curvature!

Moreover, said Newton, the moon—and for that matter, the apple, too—must pull *back* on the earth. According to his universal law, every object—even a tiny meteor far out in space—must pull on every other object. *Of course* the apple pulled the earth at the same time that the earth was pulling the apple; but the apple's pull was so weak that no one could notice it. It just seemed to "fall." Likewise, the moon pulled the earth, just as the earth pulled the moon. But the moon was comparatively much larger (larger than the apple), very far away, and in motion besides: *that* was why it could neither fly off into space nor fall into the earth. Under just the right amount of pull from the earth, it *had* to keep whirling about it.

Let us follow the basic problem that must have been churning in Newton's mind. If an object—say an apple—was as far away from the earth as the moon, how fast would it be falling around the earth, due to the earth's pull? The distance of the moon from the earth's center is about sixty times the radius of the earth itself. According to the inverse square law, then, the gravitational pull of the earth on an object which was exactly as far away as the moon would be 1/3600th of what it is on the earth's surface.

To make his calculation, Newton needed to know the exact distance to the center of the earth. But at Woolsthorpe he had no books to refer to, and his memory was faulty. He made an error, and in his figuring naturally arrived at the wrong answer—one greater by about fifteen per cent than he thought it should be.

"These two figures"—the answer he arrived at, and the answer he hoped to get—"are much too far apart," Newton thought. "This great problem is perhaps not to be solved by me. True, I could patch up my theory, yet I must deal with realities, not idle speculations. I shall lay this aside for a time."

Understandably, Newton was disappointed. If he had

known the true size of the earth it is quite likely he would have discovered the laws of gravitation sooner.

As a matter of fact, the true value of the earth's radius —the distance from its surface to its center—had been published some thirty years before.

It is curious that even when he returned to Cambridge he did nôt take the trouble to look up the correct figure and rework his mathematics. Just six years later, the French astronomer, Jean Picard, gave accurate earth measurements at a meeting of the Royal Society. In particular, Newton had needed to know what the true figure was for one degree of the earth's latitude so he could find out the earth's size. But this was not, as Newton had thought, 60 English miles, but a figure quite a bit larger than he supposed, namely, 69.1 miles. How could this have escaped Newton's notice, since Newton was present at this very meeting?

This is one of the puzzles of history. Very likely, Newton was simply being Newton. He was occupied with other matters—his optical experiments, perhaps, or alchemy. It was not until 1682, when idle conversation at the Royal Society turned to Picard's work, that Newton noted down the true figure of the earth's radius and reworked his figures.

Yet Newton said nothing of these discoveries to anyone. By sheer genius he had hit on the beginning of a great law, yet because he had made an error of fifteen per cent in an important calculation he did not dare to think that the theory forming in his mind was correct.

Was he disappointed? Of course. But beaten? No. There

were other things for him to think about in the closet-sized room at the manor house.

"This is only the beginning . . ." Isaac promised himself.

Optics

The invention of the telescope and particularly Galileo's remarkable use of it, made the study of *optics,* or the science of light, a subject of keen interest to "natural philosophers" of the seventeenth century.

Newton himself was drawn to the subject of optics in quite an ordinary manner. In 1664, as an undergraduate, he had observed and measured the moon's halos. He had ground lenses under Barrow's instruction and had listened carefully to his lectures on optics.

Early in 1666 Newton bought a prism of his own to examine light. A few years later, in his first published paper, he wrote: ". . . in the beginning of the year 1666 (at which time I applied myself to the grinding of optic glasses of other figures than spherical), I procured a triangular prism to try therewith the celebrated phenomena of colors . . ."

Newton also soon discovered why the telescopes of his day were not the best ones that could be made. That discovery was to lead him later to the invention of a practical reflecting telescope; yet he did not make this instrument until late in 1668. However, it is clear from certain of Newton's writings that his first ideas concerning the spectrum must have come to him in 1666.

Shut away in the tiny room at the Woolsthorpe manor

house, Isaac began experimenting rather idly at first with the prism he had bought. He wrote: ". . . having darkened my chamber and made a small hole in my window shutters, to let in a convenient quantity of the sun's light,

Using a prism, Newton produced the spectrum on his chamber wall.

I placed my prism at its entrance that it might thereby be refracted to the opposite wall. It was at first a very pleasant divertissement."

But Isaac soon found that what at first had been merely a "divertissement"—or amusement—was a very scientific matter indeed. The beam of sunlight he sent through the prism was bent, or refracted. It did not emerge from his prism as the same beam of white light—but as a bundle of beams made up of all colors. And each of these beams was bent at a different angle so that they pointed in different directions.

Newton, like hundreds before him, had produced the *spectrum* on his chamber wall. The individual colors were arranged with red bent the least and at the top of the band

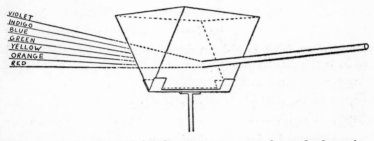

The round beam of light that Newton sent through the prism was bent so that it made a strip five times as long as it was broad.

of colors. The order of the other colors was orange, yellow, green, blue, indigo, and finally violet, which was bent the most at the bottom of the whole band. From this, it was immediately clear to Newton that a beam of white light was not *homogeneous,* that is, it was not all of one kind. It was, in Newton's own words, a "most surprising and wonderful composition,"—and mixed in "due proportion." Today we would say that each of the colors had its own individual wave length.

The beam of sunlight that Isaac had sent through the prism was one whose cross section was round. It was bent once on entering the prism, and again when it came out. The first visible result was of course that the beam was no longer white, but colored. The second—and more thought-provoking—was that the patch of colored light was now *no longer circular* but a strip *five times as long as it was broad!*

One thing was at once clear to the young thinker, who had already had some experience with the refracting telescopes of his day. Refracting telescopes depended on the use of lenses that bent light as prisms did. But if circular beams of light could be lengthened into wide colored strips, then how could an instrument, which depended upon this basic principle, help but give images that were colored and blurred?

The way young Newton was to solve this problem in the next two years was to bring his name to the lips of the most advanced scientists of his day.

SIX

Newton and the Reflecting Telescope

EARLY in the year 1667, when the bubonic plague had lessened in the English towns, Newton went back to his studies at Cambridge. His inquiring mind had been sharpened by his months of meditation at Woolsthorpe. Again he took up the work he had left undone during the plague years.

In barely a year and a half, Newton had laid down the whole foundation for the rest of his life's work. Whatever he was to do in the future would be merely an enlargement of what he had begun at Woolsthorpe. Nowhere else in the history of science can we find that so much brilliant and original thinking had been done in so short a time.

From this point on in his career, Newton was to devote ten years apiece to each of the subjects that were his main scientific concern—fluxions, gravitation, and optics. Upon his return to Cambridge until about 1678, he worked largely on his optical studies. From about 1678 to 1688, he concentrated on the still greater discovery of universal gravitation. And from 1688 to just before 1700, he developed his astronomical work and perfected his mathematics, particularly his method of fluxions.

It was like Newton, when he returned to the University, to say nothing to anyone about his discoveries. What he craved was more work, more books, more study and experiment. During this period, Issac showed himself to have the true, inquiring scientific spirit—he felt that it was useless to tell anyone what he himself was still unsure of.

His superiors at Trinity, however, recognized the young man's ability, for he was elected a Minor Fellow of Trinity only six short months after the College reopened. Not long afterward, three Major Fellowships fell vacant and Newton promptly received one of them. He could now settle down to months of hard work without serious financial worries. In a ground floor apartment next to the College chapel, he did just this.

Soon he was busy with drills and hammers, compasses and magnets, prisms and materials for polishing glass and shaping metal. He spent the Christmas holidays in Lincolnshire, but returned to Cambridge early in 1668 to take his Master of Arts degree.

During August and September of that year he went to London to buy some much-needed equipment—especially materials for his optical studies. Upon his return to his rooms at Trinity, he again took up a favorite project that he had been working on at the outbreak of the plague.

Newton set about designing the first practical reflecting telescope.

A telescope is based generally upon the following principle: an image of some distant object is formed by a lens—

called the *object lens*—and this same image is, in turn, observed by means of another lens—called the *eyepiece*. However, if the telescope is to be any good at all, the object lens must be able to collect the light rays from points of the observed object and focus them accurately. If the rays from any given point of the object do not give an exact point image, then the telescope suffers from optical confusion, or *aberration*.

It is a fact however—as Newton and others before him found out—that the only way light rays from an object point can come to an exact focus at another point is by *reflection* at a plane, or flat surface. A plane mirror, for example, will reflect an image of an object that is perfect and sharp to the last detail. But when light rays are bent or *refracted* at a flat, spherical, or elliptical surface between one medium, such as air, and another, such as glass, they give images that are blurred and indistinct.

Look at the diagram on the next page. Light rays from a source at point O are traveling through air until they hit the surface of a spherical piece of glass at points F_1, F_2, F_3, etc. After the rays enter the glass from air, each is refracted or bent. Some are bent more, some less, according to the angle at which they hit the glass. Thus we have the newly-bent rays inside the glass represented by the lines, F_1G_1, F_2G_2, F_3G_3, and so forth. Now, if you extend those new lines backward by dotted ones, they will not meet at a common point such as O—their starting point. They are now just a jumble of complicated rays that do not form any kind of sharp image at all.

This optical nuisance is called *spherical aberration*.

Because most telescopes before Newton's generation had spherical lenses, they all suffered from it. Even Galileo's famous telescope was quite a faulty instrument and the

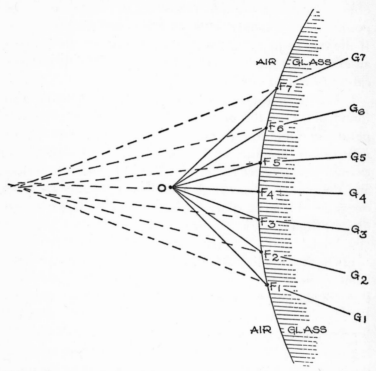

Spherical aberration. *Most telescopes before Newton's time suffered from this nuisance.*

strain of spherical aberration probably helped make Galileo blind toward the end of his life. A thorough search was being made by the scientific minds of the day to try to do away with spherical aberration.

[56]

Earlier, the great French scientist, René Descartes, thought he had solved the difficulty when he suggested that not spherical lenses were needed but elliptically shaped ones. Yet the grinding and polishing of such surfaces was a difficult, if not impossible, task in Newton's time. Even if the workmen of the day had been able to produce the lenses suggested by Descartes, there would have been little improvement on the problem.

However, it was not spherical aberration alone that lay at the heart of the difficulty. Actually the fault lay elsewhere, and not only Galileo and Descartes, but Kepler too, were unaware of this. Surely these men had observed the colors of the rainbow, the flashing quality in a soap bubble, the bluish brilliance of a lady's diamond—even the colors produced by white light passing through their own prisms. These things seemed to beg for scientific explanation, and yet the principle behind them remained unexplained until Newton gave it to the world.

At Woolsthorpe, when he was only twenty-three, Newton had begun experimenting with the prism—and had reached the startling conclusion that there *was no way* to improve the telescopes of Kepler and Galileo. Instruments would have to be built according to an entirely new idea if men were to view the heavens with anything like true exactness. For Newton had begun to realize that these early telescopes were inaccurate not only because of spherical aberration, but because of *color*.

Think back to Newton's experiment with the prism at Woolsthorpe. He had passed white light through his prism and it had broken down, by refraction, into the colors of the spectrum. Naturally the lenses of these early telescopes refracted light just as a prism did. This resulted in the blurred color fringes that annoyed Galileo and others when, for example, they focused their instruments on a distant star. Their lenses—whatever their shape—simply could not produce a sharp, clear image of the star because colors had been introduced by refraction.

Newton, however, knew that *reflection* at any surface would not produce color blurring, and he decided to give up the idea of *refracting* telescopes altogether. He would build one on the *reflection* principle. Newton was not the first to think of the idea, however. A few years before, the distinguished Scottish mathematician, James Gregory, had suggested a plan for a reflecting telescope, but had never actually made one. Also, Gregory was not acquainted with such an instrument's main advantage, namely that it would do away with the troublesome color fringes.

Alone in his rooms near the College Chapel, Isaac began shaping, with his own hands, the tiny metal mirror for the first reflecting telescope. Days were spent in polishing its concave surface—a surface that curved inward like the bowl of a spoon. The alloy from which it was formed was Newton's own—a mixture of copper, tin, and arsenic.

Isaac worked with intense enthusiasm. The telescope he finally produced was ridiculously small. It was only six inches long, with a diameter of one inch! Yet it could magnify an object forty times—and this, as Newton himself pointed out, was as much as could be expected of a refracting telescope fully six feet long!

Yet Newton faced a new problem in making his telescope. James Gregory had suggested a reflecting instrument made up of two concave mirrors facing one another. Light from the object to be observed was to be reflected from one of them to a focal point in front of the other. But how could an observer see the image unless his head were inside the telescope's tube? Gregory's idea was to have the second mirror reflect the light again, and bring it to a focus through a hole drilled in the first mirror. Here the image could be seen by an observer using an eyepiece behind the hole.

Newton realized that this was rather a clumsy arrangement. Instead, he hit on the idea of *boring a hole in the side* of the telescope's outer tube and bringing the image out by placing a small, flat metal mirror at an angle of 45° to the telescope's axis *inside* the telescope. Thus an observer using an eyepiece at the side of the instrument would catch the objects rays being thrown out sideways. Newton was the first man to use this device.

Newton's instrument was crude. The idea behind it was new. When he had finished his telescope, Newton wondered how well it would work in practice. On the first clear night the young Trinity scholar turned it skyward and thrilled. There in the tiny eyepiece were the planet Jupiter and its then-known four moons. With a little difficulty and much practice Newton was also able to observe the phases of the planet Venus. And each of these images shone bright and clear and free from annoying color fringes!

Newton made this first reflecting telescope in the year 1668. Later in 1671, he was to make a second, which would win him fame and honor all over Europe.

Today we know that in his early optical work Newton was wrong in taking two things for granted. In the first place, Isaac used a spherically ground mirror. A parabolic

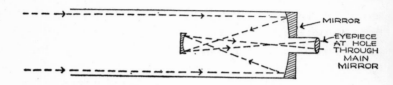

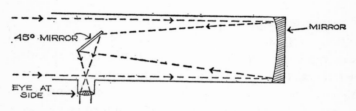

Above, James Gregory's suggestion for a reflecting telescope. Below, the principle of Newton's reflecting telescope.

one—one shaped like an automobile headlight—would have given a truer image of the heavenly bodies. In the second place, Newton took it for granted that whatever the shapes of the lenses used in telescopes, they would always produce fringes of color. If the same kind of glass is used throughout, Newton was perfectly right. Actually, by combining certain types of glass in just the right way, the various colors produced by refraction can be "strained out" of a modern lens.

The fact remains, however, that the most advanced telescopes in use today—the 100-inch mirror telescope at Mount Wilson and the 200-inch instrument at Mount Palomar—are reflecting telescopes just as Newton's was. And if you purchase any good amateur telescope today, the chances are you will find the eyepiece somewhere on the side of the tube, where young Newton first placed his in 1668.

SEVEN

Newton Wins a Professorship—and Fame

WHILE he was working out the design of his reflecting telescope, other things were also happening to the young Cambridge Fellow.

Newton had long been under the excellent tutorship of Dr. Isaac Barrow. The Lucasian Professor of Mathematics had seriously been considering giving up his Chair in favor of a younger man. Besides being a brilliant scientist, Dr. Barrow was also a man who was deeply interested in advanced religious ideas. Soon he hoped to resign his position at the University to devote himself entirely to his religious work.

Naturally enough, he thought of his brilliant young assistant as a possible candidate for the Lucasian Chair—and for two good reasons. The first was that Newton had given him invaluable help in preparing his lectures on optics for publication in 1669. The second—and considerably better basis for judging Newton's ability—was a paper that the young man had submitted to Barrow in that same year.

This manuscript was entitled *On Analysis of Equations*

with an Infinite Number of Terms. Sometimes it is called simply *De Analysi*—the shortened form of its Latin title, since most scholarly work of the time was written in that language. This paper was the first written statement of Newton's mathematical discoveries, particularly on fluxions, ever to find its way into another man's hands.

Soon after submitting this work to Barrow, Newton seemed to have forgotten the whole matter. He was deep in his telescope project now and, for the time being, the manuscript no longer interested him. It interested Barrow a great deal, however. Newton had suggested—and Barrow agreed—that it might be sent to John Collins. Collins was a mathematician who exchanged frequent letters with other mathematicians, and acted as a sort of clearing house between them.

Barrow was excited about Newton's work, and sent an enthusiastic letter to John Collins on July 31, 1669. He wrote: "A friend of mine here, that hath an excellent genius to these things, brought me . . . papers . . . which I suppose will please you."

Newton, however, had not wanted to tell anyone that he was the author of *De Analysi*. He was shy and wished only to be let alone to work; he saw no point in attaching his name to his scientific accomplishments. The work had been done, and that was that. Now he must proceed with other matters.

But a few days later, Barrow must have succeeded in changing his modest young assistant's mind, because he wrote to Collins: "I am glad my friend's paper gives you so much satisfaction; his name is Mr. Newton, a Fellow of our college, and very young (being but the second year Master of Arts), but of an extraordinary genius and proficiency in these things."

John Collins was as excited about Newton's work as Barrow. He returned Newton's original paper to the Lucasian Professor, but made copies to send to the outstanding mathematicians in England and on the continent of Europe. The great German mathematician, Gottfried von Leibnitz, wrote that he would like to know more about the youthful Trinity scholar's method of calculating the areas of curves.

Not long after this, John Collins sent along to Newton a number of difficult problems that had puzzled the best minds in London. Much to Collins' delight, Newton quickly solved them.

The contents of *De Analysi,* however, was not to be published until 1711—some forty-two years later! Why? Newton himself was about to plunge into his telescope project. In his usual way, he probably pigeonholed the manuscript —satisfied that the problem had been solved and that there were other things to be done.

Barrow and Collins were more experienced men than Newton, but they evidently did not realize how important it was to publish the paper—both for the advancement of knowledge and for Newton's own reputation. Probably Barrow's mind was most occupied with his optical publications as well as his coming retirement.

At any rate, the failure to put this important work into print at once was to cause Newton trouble later. For at the same time he was developing the calculus, so was

Leibnitz. As the years went on, there would develop a bitter dispute between the two men as to which one had been the first inventor of the calculus.

Meanwhile, all doubt as to who would be his successor left Barrow's mind. Newton's brilliance—at least at Cambridge—had become fully recognized. On October 29, 1669, he was appointed Lucasian Professor of Mathematics, at a salary of about one hundred pounds a year. This, in addition to the income he received as a Fellow of the University, brought his total living up to about two hundred pounds a year. In Newton's day, this was a comfortable sum of money.

Isaac could scarcely believe his good fortune. At the early age of twenty-seven he had been appointed to one of the world's most famous professorships. In addition, his duties were not too demanding. As Lucasian Professor, he was required to deliver only one lecture a week, and to meet with his students twice weekly to talk over any problems they might have. This schedule left him ample time for his own studies and experiments.

Newton decided to lecture on optics because he was then in the middle of further research on the spectrum. Each week he laid before his students the results of his studies, speaking in a slow, almost mumbling voice that had nothing in it of drama and liveliness.

Often no students showed up at all, whereupon Newton would gather up his notes and return to his experiments. Even when students did show up to hear Professor Newton, they found it hard to understand fully what he was saying. For in these lectures Newton spent little time on simple, basic principles; he went directly to his latest findings—perhaps those he had reached a day or two before. He did not seem an exciting person—a quiet man of middle

Newton lecturing before his students at Cambridge.

height, prominent chin and nose, and receding hairline—and probably many of the students dozed as he droned on before them.

So the year 1669 passed. Then 1670. Newton still worked on his telescope from time to time. By 1671, however, the original telescope seems to have disappeared. To Newton it was not a great loss, since he considered it a very crude instrument. Yet so many of his fellow-workers at Cambridge expressed interest in the reflecting telescope that Newton made a second and then a third.

About this time the Royal Society began to hear of Newton's fame as a telescope maker. The Society soon sent a request to Newton to send them one of his instruments for inspection. Isaac replied that he would be glad to do so.

The instrument Newton sent up to the Society that same year was about nine inches long, with a mirror about two inches across. The telescope was applauded by the Royal Society and excited its members' interest and admiration. Today this same instrument is one of the Society's most valued possessions.

Newton constructed still another model of his telescope and this was seen and admired by the London public in 1671. King Charles II and other important persons were invited to look through the little instrument that performed better than others twice and even three times its size.

Newton's fame was spreading. Educated men everywhere were beginning to ask about the brilliant, young Cambridge Fellow.

Among the first to award him public honor for his work was the Royal Society itself. He was at once suggested for membership in that famous body, and was elected without delay on January 11, 1672.

Thus, when he had barely passed thirty, Isaac Newton had "arrived." It was to be but the beginning of a long and well-spent lifetime of contribution to science.

EIGHT

A Paper on Light—
and Newton's Opponent

PLEASED at his election to the Royal Society, Isaac promptly offered to make known to its members what, to him, was something far more valuable than a reflecting telescope.

This was a paper on his discoveries about the spectrum and the nature of color. At last, Newton himself was excited about telling the public of his scientific findings.

When the paper was finished, Newton sent it to Henry Oldenburg, Secretary of the Royal Society, on February 6, 1672. Soon after this, it was published in the *Philosophical Transactions,* the official record of the Royal Society. The title of Newton's first published work was *The Composition of White Light.*

By this time the young Cambridge Fellow had reached more definite conclusions about that mysterious five-times extension of white light when a beam was passed through a prism.

At first Isaac had looked for quite impossible explanations of this phenomenon. Soon it dawned on him that there must be a number of different colors making up the now-extended single beam, and that each of these had been bent differently by refraction through the prism. He also found that the patch of colors could be turned back into white light again—and the cross-section restored to its original circular shape—by passing the colored patch through a second prism of exactly the same shape.

By experimenting with light falling on this and that portion of the colored patch produced by his prism, Newton proved beyond doubt that these lights were different from each other—that each suffered a different degree of refraction, or bending, when passed through the prism. The colors that were bent the least lay at the red end of the spectrum, while those bent the most lay at the violet end. White light, then, was not *homogeneous*—consisting of itself alone—but was made up of differently colored rays. Moreover, once one of the colors of the spectrum had been separated from white light, it could not *itself* be broken up or changed in any way.

Newton went even further. He wrote that the color of a thing was due to the light by which the thing *is seen,* and not the thing itself. Thus when we say that an apple is red, we mean that the apple gives back the red rays of the light striking it. In other words, it reflects red light to our eyes but absorbs or soaks up the rest of the colors of the spectrum.

These, in part, were the ideas contained in the paper Newton presented to the Royal Society. So important and revolutionary did this information seem that the Society immediately appointed a committee to judge just how valuable it was. A member of this committee was

Robert Hooke, who himself wrote the report on Newton's findings. Although Hooke and the rest of the committee spoke highly of Newton's work, Hooke had some doubts about it and did not mind saying so. This man was to be a thorn in Newton's side for many years to come.

Hooke was older than Newton and had won a reputation as a great inventor. Among his many inventions were a device for measuring the moisture in the atmosphere, a clock-driven telescope for following the stars, a rain gauge, and the spiral watch spring. Robert Hooke also devised improvements for clocks, watches, and telescopes, and even made some of the first practical advances in the science of sound. Students today become acquainted with his name through *Hooke's Law,* which states that the stress on a body is in direct proportion to the strain. He also invented what today is known as the universal joint, sometimes still called *Hooke's joint.* As if this were not enough, Hooke's brilliance also led him to important discoveries concerning the cell structure of plants, telegraphy, and fossil remains as records of past ages. He was also a good architect.

Hooke was indeed a man who had knowledge of a surprising number of things. The trouble was, however, that he tended to have so many ideas that he could not develop them all fully. Also, Hooke had had a difficult personal life; he was sickly, proud, and irritable. Interested in all things but seldom bringing any of them to full completion, he was suspicious of any other scientists who brought forth ideas that clashed with his own.

Probably jealous of the younger man's brilliant explanations before the Royal Society, Hooke, in the matter of Newton's telescope, said that in 1664 he himself had "made a little tube of about an inch long for my fob, which performed more than any telescope of fifty feet after the common manner." Hooke, however, went on to say that he had not bothered to improve on this little pocket model telescope because he had been too busy with other matters. Ever suspicious, he also said that he had been afraid that London "glass grinders" might steal his secret from him!

A year or so later, upon the publication of Newton's paper, Hooke again criticized Newton. True, he praised the "niceness and curiosity" of Newton's experiments, but disagreed with Newton's conclusions. In this attack, Hooke suggested that the younger man ought to stick to his telescope-making while leaving the more important matter of theories of light to his elders. In a later attack, Hooke not only disagreed with Newton's theories but went so far as to suggest that several of Newton's ideas on light had actually originated with himself, Hooke!

But Newton proved that he could be as effective with a pen as with a prism. During the weeks that followed he answered Hooke's objections point by point and—at first—good-naturedly. In one of his replies, Newton wrote: "Mr. Hooke thinks himself concerned to reprehend me for laying aside the thoughts of improving optics by refraction. But he knows well it is not for one man to prescribe rules to the studies of another, especially not without understanding the grounds on which he proceeds."

Newton had other critics as well as Robert Hooke. In the matter of the five-fold extension of the beam of color, a man named Lucas of the city of Liége in Belgium claimed to have performed the same experiment, obtaining an extension of only three and one-half times! Both men insisted doggedly that their results were correct. What neither suspected, however, was that each had used a different kind of glass for his prism. And different types of glass could scatter light to different degrees during refraction.

Another critic was a French priest named Ignatius Pardies. After an exchange of letters, Pardies apologized to Newton for having misunderstood his theories. In this time of personal trial, Newton took the time to reply to Pardies with courtesy, tact, and in a true scientific spirit: "For the safest and best method of philosophizing we should . . . first inquire diligently into the properties of things . . . establishing these properties by experiment, and then to proceed more slowly . . . for the explanation of them."

Criticism came from still other men. Christian Huygens, the great Dutch scientist, had also raised objections to Newton's work; so had Descartes and the Italian, Grimaldi. A particularly annoying critic was another Belgian named Linus, an ignorant, uninformed man who had printed some absurd things about Newton's work on light.

Newton hated these petty disputes. They came to weigh more and more heavily on him as the years went by. His gloomy state of mind in 1676 was clear when he wrote these well-known words to Oldenburg: "I see I have made myself a slave to philosophy, but if I get free of Mr. Linus' business I will resolutely bid adieu to it eternally, excepting what I do for my own satisfaction, or leave to come out after me; for I see a man must resolve to put out nothing new, or become a slave to defend it."

The shy Trinity professor had received his first real blows from the outside world. He had been hurt, and hurt seriously. Aside from feeling that his critics were merely bringing up unimportant objections about his work, Newton had always disliked criticism, and even more had disliked publicity. In the famous quotation to Oldenburg above, he clearly says that he would no longer have his name associated with published accounts of his work. What further pained Newton was that he had been accused of stealing another man's ideas.

The worldly Barrow probably talked many times to Newton during this difficult period, encouraging and comforting him. His old roommate, John Wickens, must also have comforted him. Visits from time to time to Woolsthorpe manor house may also have relieved his mind of the dispute his first published paper had touched off.

Still, deep scars had been left on Newton by the outside world. He decided to stop wasting his all-important energy on answering his critics. He would now work alone, if only "for his own satisfaction." During the next few years, then, Isaac Newton turned his back on the world.

"The less I hear of it, the better," he resolved. "Besides, there are so many more things to learn about . . ."

NINE

Newton Faces a Crisis

D URING the next few years scraps of letters and reports
of close friends shows that the Cambridge professor
led the life of a typical bachelor. He was far from the
comfort and care of a mother; he had never married.
Whatever required doing he did clumsily for himself;
he lived only for the work in which he was engaged.

From his youth on, Newton had never remembered
to eat regularly. He was also careless about his health,
although he was fond of dosing himself with homemade
remedies of his own. One of these was " . . . orange peel
boiled in water, which he drank as tea, sweetened with
sugar, and taken with bread and butter." Many nights he
worked till well past midnight, missing precious hours
of restful sleep. At the age of thirty, Newton was already
turning gray.

But Newton had also won a reputation among his friends
as a kindly and devout man—an influence for good in
many ways. He was as ready to advise a student how he
should act when insulted, as he was to lend a friend—
or even a stranger—a pound or two. Throughout his life
Newton was known for being very free with his money.

He gave generous gifts and loans to friends and relatives. He also spent money freely on himself, especially for items of scientific equipment.

Yet while it was true that from both his Trinity Fellowship and the Lucasian Chair, Newton earned enough to meet his needs, he was faced with the threat of a financial setback early in 1675.

Soon after he had given up the Lucasian Chair, Dr. Barrow was appointed Master of Trinity College. Newton, together with others who had Trinity's best interests at heart, rejoiced. Before Barrow's appointment, many laws of the College had not been strictly enforced. Here and there bad practices had crept in. Dr. Barrow was a man who could do away with laxity and neglect, and supervise Trinity as its founders originally intended.

The trouble was that, in beginning his reforms, Barrow realized that sooner or later he would have to hurt Newton. Normally a Trinity Fellowship was good for a period of seven years. During this time a Fellow was expected to study religious subjects thoroughly so that he could eventually take holy orders and become a clergyman. Actually, however, many Fellows stayed on far longer at the University, preferring the income from their Fellowships and the university life to that of a low-paid parish clergyman.

Not only had Newton not taken holy orders, but his seven-year Fellowship was about to run out. Thus he would have to live on the salary of the Lucasian Chair alone. Under the revival of the old University rule, Newton would lose his Fellowship unless he agreed to take holy orders.

Barrow knew where his duty lay, but still he hesitated. He had no wish to upset Newton, or to interrupt his experiments. The former Lucasian Professor must have paced the College quadrangle a good many nights before he could bring himself to mount what is known today as "Newton's staircase," just off the Great Court.

Barrow knew what he would find in Newton's rooms— a scarcely-touched dinner on the table, a still-full goblet of ale, books and sheafs of notes lying about everywhere, and Newton himself, haggard-eyed from lack of sleep, but doggedly at work on some problem. And, likely as not, his coat would be stained with chemicals from his laboratory in the garden.

But Barrow had no choice. The day came when he told Newton, as gently as he could, that even a Fellow who had been appointed to a famous Professorship would have to take holy orders at the end of his seven-year period.

Newton was deeply disturbed when he heard this news. He did not reply right away; he wrestled with the question for days before giving Barrow his decision.

Perhaps in his heart, Barrow was prepared for the answer that Newton gave him: "I cannot take holy orders, Dr. Barrow. For others, it may be the course to follow. As for me, I believe I can serve God better by not being formally bound to the church."

Why did Newton refuse to take holy orders? Certainly he believed in the fundamentals of religion, for he wrote extensively on the Bible and other religious matters. Yet it is clear that Newton wanted the same freedom in his religious life that he enjoyed in his scientific experiments.

Barrow understood. He knew that Newton was a deeply religious man for they had spent many hours together studying the early history of Christianity.

"Very well, Mr. Newton," said the Master of Trinity. "Let us say no more about the matter for the time being. I believe we can devise other means for getting round this matter."

Dr. Barrow was as good as his word. He drew up a petition to the Crown—copies of which were sent to the proper authorities—requesting that an exception be made in the case of such a brilliant man as Newton. After all, King Charles himself was interested in science; perhaps he would look favorably on Newton's case.

In due course, Newton went to London to await his hearing before the Royal Court.

Full of doubt about whether the king would agree to this special arrangement, Newton spent five anxious weeks in London. Much of this time he waited about in the outside offices of important people whose aid he needed for his petition.

The fashionable London of the day, with its elaborate court life, meant little to the Cambridge professor. Neither the lace-ruffled dandies at court, nor the hoop-skirted ladies who accompanied them, were Newton's kind of people. Outside the fashionable drawing rooms the filthy streets contained gangs of roving ruffians who made it dangerous for decent citizens to go out at night. Busy coffeehouses were everywhere, packed with business and professional men exchanging the latest gossip.

To all of this Newton was only an onlooker. He was worried and uneasy about his petition and thinking about unfinished problems back at Trinity. Yet as the days went by the Cambridge professor was pleasantly surprised to discover that his name meant something to people. Perhaps, he decided, it was good that he had taken this London trip. At Trinity, he had been too much alone. Newton decided to make the most of his stay in the city; afterward he would return to his work refreshed.

He began to attend the regular Wednesday meetings of the Royal Society. Henry Oldenburg, the Society's Secretary, was overjoyed to see him. Some time before, Newton, more and more worried about his finances, had rather childishly written to Oldenburg threatening to resign from the Royal Society. As his reason, Newton had complained that the distance between Cambridge and London was too great for him to attend the weekly meetings. Actually it was the shilling per week dues that Newton thought of saving!

At any rate, Oldenburg understood and, fearful of losing Newton's membership, proposed to the Society that "Mr. Newton . . . be excused from the weekly payments." Not only was Newton excused from these payments, but so were others—including Newton's old opponent, Robert Hooke!

Although he had been a member of the Royal Society for many months, Newton attended his first formal meetings during his stay in London. Oldenburg saw to it that

Newton met everyone worth meeting. His name seemed to carry weight with the other members. Soon the news of why he had come to London was known to all of them.

Newton attending his first formal meeting of the Royal Society in London.

On every side, he received assurances that King Charles II would grant his petition.

At last, on March 12, 1675, a grateful and relieved Newton learned that King Charles had indeed signed an arrangement for him. It stated that Newton might keep his Fellowship at Trinity without entering holy order for *as long as* he remained Lucasian Professor of Mathematics!

Overjoyed, Newton returned to Cambridge to tell Barrow the good news—and to get down to serious work again.

TEN

The Importance of Newton's Work on Light

GREATLY encouraged now, Isaac Newton continued his work and toward the end of 1675 wrote again to his friend Oldenburg, offering to send the Royal Society another paper on the nature of color and light. The important paper was accepted by the Society late in December; in it is contained much of Newton's major work on optics.

Newton was still his old self, however. He would not allow Oldenburg to print his paper in the Society's *Transactions* until he had completed further experiments. But it was read at two later meetings of the Royal Society and was enthusiastically received by the members.

In that paper and in Newton's later work on light were important contributions that have greatly influenced our modern world.

Newton's discovery of the spectrum alone was one of the most significant in the history of science. It has led to striking developments in all branches of knowledge. The discovery of the presence of black lines in the light from the sun—called *Fraunhofer lines* after their German discoverer—led directly to *spectral analysis,* which has revolutionized physics, chemistry, and astronomy. By analyzing the distant light of the stars with an instrument called a *spectroscope* scientists can find out what material they are made of, whether they are moving toward or away from us, and approximately how far away they are.

Newton's pioneer work on the spectrum also led to the work of Niels Bohr and other investigators who later were to throw much light on just what makes up the matter of the universe. Likewise, Max Planck's brilliant Quantum Theory of the late nineteenth century owes a great debt of gratitude to Newton's preliminary work on the spectrum.

Newton not only used the reflecting principle in the telescope, he also applied it to the microscope as well. He further made a suggestion that when using ordinary refracting-type microscopes, light of only one color—*monochromatic* light—be used, a technique practiced in modern laboratories today.

Also, while working with the 45-degree metal mirror on his own reflecting telescope, Newton realized how imperfect the reflection from a metal surface was bound to be. He thus hit on an idea without which modern high-powered binoculars would be impossible. This was simply that in view of the high refractive ability of glass, a perfect right-angled *glass prism* could be used to bend light, giving much better results than metal surfaces.

Newton also made discoveries of great theoretical importance in connection with the colors produced in thin films of transparent matter, as in flakes of mica and soap bubbles. Some of these thin films of material produced one set of colors and others a different set. He experimented with these color phenomena by holding lenses at different distances from flat plates of glass and other materials that transmitted light. First circles of color, and then ones of darkness were produced. These alternating rings, which have great meaning in modern laboratory research, are called "Newton's rings." The method by which Newton made calculations of these rings is also used by today's scientists.

These experiments led Newton to the early conclusion that a given ray of light—any ray—could not have exactly the same properties at all points along its length. There had to be certain variations and Newton called these "fits." Newton did not pretend to understand why these should exist in light rays, but the very fact that they did caused him to state a theory of light that was opposed by nearly all of the scientists of his time.

In general, Newton considered light to consist of very tiny particles given forth by luminous (glowing) bodies in space, like the sun or the stars. This "particle theory" is sometimes called the *Corpuscular Theory,* since corpuscles are very small particles.

Opposing this theory was one put forward by Christian Huygens. Robert Hooke and many others also favored Huygens' theory. Huygens believed that light, much like sound, was a form of wave motion. He said that the different parts of a light wave set up an infinite number of secondary waves. In time, these secondary waves reinforced each other to produce new waves. Huygens thought that in this way light was *propagated,* or carried along.

But Huygens also believed that these waves had to have a special medium through which to move. Since light rays could pass through a vacuum, however, he felt that this medium could not be air. So, Huygens assumed the presence of an all-pervading, mysterious substance called "ether." Through this medium, rays of light were supposed to be transmitted. Today scientists believe that there is no such substance as the ether Huygens described.

The fact that Newton did not insist on the correctness of his own particle theory is proof of his scientific honesty. He even believed in a kind of "ether" of his own—though it was unlike that of Huygens.

Years later, when he was an old man and a friend told him of some astronomical observations that went against Newtonian theory, Newton replied: "It may be so, there is no arguing against facts and experiments."

This was exactly Newton's attitude concerning the two opposing theories of light—his and Huygens'. Never one to insist on his own opinions, he realized perfectly that both served to explain the nature of light equally well. He tended however to doubt the wave theory on two counts: the presence of the mysterious ether could not be proved; and the wave theory could not account for the fact that light seemed to travel in perfectly straight lines.

During his own century and the next, Newton's influence on scientific thought was so great that the particle theory was believed to be correct. But in the nineteenth century, due to the work of Thomas Young and Augustin Fresnel, the wave theory gained favor.

The amazing thing is, however, that in recent years men of science everywhere seem to be agreed that light rays exhibit *both* particle properties *and* wave properties— a conclusion that Isaac Newton had reached in the mid-seventeenth century!

ELEVEN

Gravitation Again

THE YEARS between 1676 and 1679 Newton spent quietly in his own studies at Trinity. Still avoiding society, Newton gave his friends the impression that he was engaged in unimportant work such as alchemy. But he was really living a life of great scientific excitement within himself.

True, Newton spent much time in the chemical laboratory in his garden, but his lectures were on subjects that interested him most. He was now exchanging letters with Leibnitz on his methods of mathematical analysis. He also took part in various University functions and began deep studies of the Bible, probably due to Barrow's influence.

The year 1677, however, brought double sadness to Newton. First Isaac Barrow died, and a few months later he was followed by Henry Oldenburg. Each of these men, in his own way, had meant much to Newton. The lonely Lucasian Professor had doubtless thought of them as his best friends.

The brilliant, yet erratic, Robert Hooke succeeded Oldenburg as Secretary of the Royal Society in the year 1678. Although the two men had had their differences in the past, Hooke nevertheless wrote a polite letter to Newton late in November of 1679, asking if he had anything of scientific interest to send to the Royal Society. Newton had been silent for some time on scientific matters, even though Society members asked frequently for new findings.

In a friendly enough manner, Hooke also asked Newton's opinion of a new method of planetary motions suggested by the Frenchman, Mallement de Messanges.

Newton, determined to show that there was no longer any bitterness on his part, answered Hooke's letter with a friendly one of his own. Not only did he give his opinion of Messanges' planetary theories, but Newton decided to "bury the hatchet" by suggesting a little scientific puzzle to Hooke. Newton knew that Hooke loved a problem as well as he himself did; perhaps it would also please the Royal Society.

The problem had to do with the earth's daily rotation on its axis once every twenty-four hours. This problem was unusual in that no one had ever given direct proof of the earth's rotation—except in *indirectly* proving it by observation of the changing positions of the sun and the stars.

Newton of course knew that as the earth rotates, everything rotated along with it—people, houses, trees, the oceans. But how could this supposed rotation be distinguished from what appeared to be a state of rest on the earth's surface? Thus, if a ball is thrown straight up in the air, it falls back into the thrower's hands. If a man jumps straight up in the air, he falls directly back to the spot he jumped from. This happens because of gravity that seems to pull objects straight downward in a vertical line which, if extended, would pass through the center of the earth.

But where, Newton asked, is there any direct evidence of the fact that every object on earth is actually whirling about in a great circle at hundreds of miles an hour? Nothing on the earth *seems* to move because *everything is moving* in the same system!

But what about an object very high above the earth and therefore farther from the earth's center? Say a stone fixed to the top of an imaginary flagpole extending straight upward for many miles? Obviously the stone at the top of the flagpole, in an equal amount of time, would have to be traveling faster to cover its greater arc many miles up than, say, a man standing at the foot of the pole. This is the same as saying that the tread of an automobile tire is really moving faster and farther than the rim of the hub cap near the center of the wheel.

Carrying Newton's reasoning to the flagpole example, suppose that the stone suddenly dropped from the top of the pole directly toward the ground many miles below. Such a stone would not strike the ground directly beneath it; as Newton wrote, it would "not descend in the perpendicular . . . but, outrunning parts of the earth, will shoot forward to the east . . . describing in its fall a spiral line . . ."

Newton went on to explain in the letter to Hooke that the stone would have a greater circular speed before it is released than something on the ground directly below it. And, since the earth moved from west to east, the stone "in outrunning" the earth below it would land somewhere *east* of the straight line between it and the earth's center.

Hooke received Newton's letter and was fascinated with the suggested experiment. So much so that he read it before a meeting of the Royal Society, whose members at once appointed Hooke himself to carry out the experiment. In doing so, however, Hooke examined the matter more carefully and came to the conclusion that Newton was not quite right!

Hooke's conclusion was correct. Newton's argument, it was true, was flawless if the stone were dropped directly toward a point on the earth's *equator,* but what if it were dropped at some point in the northern hemisphere—say in *London?* In such a case, Hooke said, the stone would not drop only to the east, but a little to the south as well— or *southeast.* Hooke further claimed that such a falling body would not describe a spiral path as Newton had written but one more nearly elliptical.

Even though Hooke and Newton had agreed before-hand to keep their future differences private, Hooke could not now resist the golden opportunity of "showing up" Newton. At the next meeting of the Society, Hooke pointed out what he believed to be Newton's errors.

When the experiment was actually carried out, Hooke's direction of southeast proved to be the right one for the falling body. The Secretary now took every opportunity to show that Newton was ignorant of the true laws of gravitation.

Newton, of course, was not only angry with Hooke, but with himself as well for a careless calculation. Newton generously admitted his error by writing to Hooke. Yes, such a falling body in the vicinity of London would fall to the southeast, but Newton suspected that, while Hooke

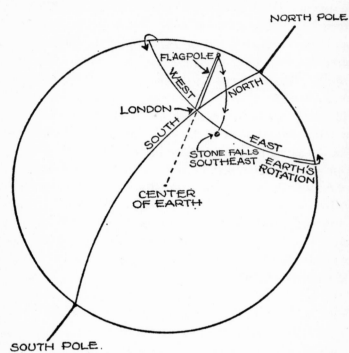

Proof of the earth's rotation. A falling body in a northern latitude would strike the earth south and east of its circle of latitude.

was also right about its elliptical path, he could not prove it.

Newton had this to say about the matter: "And though his (Hooke's) correcting my spiral occasioned my finding the theorum, by which I afterwards examined the ellipsis:

yet I am not beholden to him for any light into the business, but only for the diversion he gave me from my other studies to think on these things . . ."

True, Hooke had gained a momentary triumph, but the entire business had directed Newton toward an original train of thought that was to lead directly to Book I of his great work, the *Principia!*

Hooke himself could not prove what he stated. Actually it was Newton who was the true discoverer, for he was able to give mathematical *proof* that a body moving under gravitational attraction toward a point, varying as the inverse square of the distance from that point, describes an *ellipse* with one focus at the center of attraction. In the case of the falling stone, that focus was of course the earth's center.

Newton's mastermind had supplied the first proof of one of the great laws of the universe! It only remained for him now to go ahead and complete the entire theory of the solar system!

Yet what did Newton do? Typically, and in his own words, he "threw the calculations by, being upon other studies." By "throwing by" he probably meant that he shoved these earth-shaking notes away in some drawer and forgot about them! At the time he was at work on an alloy for one of his metal mirrors.

Was the alloy more important to Newton than the calculations upon which his greatest fame was to rest? Apparently so, for there the matter lay until a young astronomer named Edmund Halley asked about it five years later.

TWELVE

A Coffeehouse Bet

EVEN though Robert Hooke had again aroused Newton's interest in gravitational matters, one unsolved problem still bothered Newton. He could not forget his failure at Woolsthorpe to explain the moon's movement due to the earth's gravity. His calculations had been in error by about fifteen per cent.

Although the best scientific minds of the day were concerning themselves with how the *planets* moved, it was the *moon's* motion that puzzled Newton. "How," he kept asking himself, "can I hope to explain the motions of the planets when I cannot even explain the true motion of the moon around the earth? The principle underlying both must be the same. But since my previous calculations are off, I have little right to name my universal gravitation as the cause of planetary motion."

As we have seen, Newton's attention, for one reason or another, had never been drawn to the right figure for the earth's radius. Alone at Woolsthorpe in 1666, he had taken the value of 60 English miles to one degree of the earth's latitude. The correct value, as worked out by the Frenchman Picard, was much more than this—69.1 miles.

Finally, in 1682—some sixteen years later—Newton became aware of Picard's measurements. In June of that year, at a meeting of the Royal Society, the discussion turned to Picard's work. At once, Newton realized that the new figure might very well account for his error.

So excited did he become that he rushed back to Cambridge to recalculate his Woolsthorpe figures. As he worked, it became more and more apparent that this new answer was the right one. Newton became so excited that he was forced to call in a friend to complete the details of the arithmetic.

The truth was now clear to Newton: the force that drags an apple to the earth is the same that pulls the moon around the earth. Moreover, he now had invented the mathematical machinery to solve the larger problem of the motions of the planets around the sun.

Toward the middle of 1682 Newton made these all-important calculations based on the law of inverse squares —a planet twice as far away from a central body like the sun was influenced by one-fourth the gravitational force, and so on. What, then, was the shape of the curved path— or orbit—of such a planet as it journeyed around its central attracting force, the sun?

Newton finally had the answer! His equations showed that the planet's orbit had to be *an ellipse.*

Here Newton had solved one of the greatest problems astronomy had ever had to face. Yet what did he do with the solution? Did he hurry to tell the Royal Society? Did he make plans for publishing his findings? Newton did neither! He shoved the calculations away in a drawer with some other notes and said nothing to anyone. The problem had been solved; it no longer interested him.

Fortunately for science, however, three other men were also trying to solve the same problem—Sir Christopher Wren, Edmund Halley, and Newton's old opponent, Robert Hooke, Secretary of the Royal Society.

On a January afternoon in 1684, these three men met in one of London's busy coffeehouses to discuss the matter.

The eldest of the three was Sir Christopher Wren, perhaps the best known architect of his time and also a fine mathematician. Wren had drawn plans for the reconstruction of London after the Great Fire in the plague year of 1666; since 1670 he had been at work on his greatest masterpiece, London's famous St. Paul's Cathedral.

Halley, twelve years younger than Newton, was fast earning a reputation as a brilliant astronomer and physicist. Besides having done important work on the motions of comets, he was deeply interested in the problems of gravitation. Earlier that same month he had worked out from Kepler's Third Law that the sun's gravitational influence varies according to the inverse square law. About the same time Hooke, too, had apparently come to the same conclusion. These two men had finally done the same thing that Newton had done in the year 1666.

Excited by his discovery, Halley had arranged to meet with these older men. He had failed in trying to solve the larger question of just what sort of path a moving body—say a planet—would follow when moving under gravitational influence. Young Halley eagerly placed the problem before the other two.

[94]

Despite his keen mathematical mind, Sir Christopher shrugged and admitted that the answer to Halley's problem was beyond him. True, he had often wondered what

Sir Christopher Wren proposes the famous "coffeehouse bet" to Robert Hooke and Edmund Halley.

the orbit of such a body might be, but he had no solution— much less proof of one.

The ever-mysterious Hooke hedged. The laws governing the motions of the heavenly bodies he said, could be demonstrated perfectly well, and furthermore he himself had done it! But it is doubtful whether Hooke had done any such thing. Brilliant but vain, he was perhaps playing for time in which to work out a solution later.

Sir Christopher then held up his hand for silence and proposed a friendly bet. He would set a time limit of two months for either Hooke or Halley to furnish not only the answer to the problem, but mathematical proof of it as well. He himself would offer a reward to the winner.

"Whoever is the first to supply this proof," said Wren, "will not only have won a great honor, but he shall also receive from me a book worth forty shillings."

Today, a forty-shilling book seems little enough payment for solving one of the greatest puzzles of astronomy, but in Newton's day forty shillings was a lot of money—and books were highly prized.

The touchy Hooke again spoke up.

"I tell you I have the answer," insisted the Secretary of the Royal Society, "but it must be kept concealed for some time—others trying for it and failing will know how to value it when I do make it public."

Winter turned to spring, and spring to summer, yet Hooke still did not fulfill his boast. In August, Halley grew tired of waiting and made up his mind to speak to the one man in England who might be able to supply the answer to the problem—Isaac Newton.

Accordingly, he made the trip to Cambridge and, with little delay, asked Newton point-blank: "Sir, what would be the path of a planet under the attraction of gravity varying inversely as the square of the distance?"

Newton replied at once and without hesitation: "An ellipse."

"But," objected Halley, "how can you know?"

"Because I have calculated it," replied Newton simply.

Halley was amazed. At once, he asked to see Newton's calculations. These, of course, were the very calculations that Newton had "thrown by" almost five years ago. In fact, so well had Newton "thrown them by" that rummage as he would among his litter of notes, he could not locate his original figures.

Newton apologized to the younger man, and offered to recalculate the entire proof again. He would then send it on to Halley in London.

As good as his word, Newton forwarded his reworked calculations to Halley three months after the latter's visit to Cambridge. The young astronomer was overjoyed. This, he decided, was the work of a mastermind. Newton's genius had remained hidden for too long. This, as well as the man's other works, should be published for the benefit of all mankind.

But a still greater surprise was in store for Halley when he revisited Newton a short time later. Newton happened to mention a brief work he had prepared on motion. The manuscript was titled *Concerning the Motions of Bodies*—or in Latin, *De Motu Corporum.*

Running his eye over the manuscript, Halley was amazed. Here was not only the detailed solution and proof of the planetary ellipse problem, but an expansion of those proofs to include the behavior of all matter in outer space!

Then and there began Edmund Halley's personal campaign to set Newton's name and work before the scientific world. He urged, begged, and pleaded with Newton to send *De Motu* to the Royal Society at once. Amused, perhaps even pleased, at the younger man's enthusiasm, Newton promised to do so. On December 10, 1684 it was read and praised by that body.

It was only the beginning. The indifferent Newton had met a man who—himself a brilliant mathematician and astronomer—realized fully the extreme importance of Newton's work. Indeed, Edmund Halley was one of those rare people in history—a great man in his own right, yet one who gladly recognized another greater than himself.

—◆—

THIRTEEN

Work on the *Principia* Begins

——◆◆◆——

Isaac Newton was now forty-two years old and at the very peak of his scientific genius. Largely at the urging of Halley and other members of the Royal Society, he was ready in the middle of 1685 to begin the writing of a work that has been called the greatest single product of one human mind.

Newton's masterwork was to be called, in its full Latin title, *Philosophiae Naturalis Principia Mathematica* ("Mathematical Principles of Natural Philosophy"). To scientists and laymen alike, however, it is always referred to simply as the *Principia*.

In the Middle Ages and even later, men of science, for various superstitious reasons, considered the number seven to have a special meaning. But Isaac Newton's "magic number" seems to have been not seven, but *eighteen*. His astonishingly great creative period at Woolsthorpe had lasted just about eighteen months. Likewise, he was to turn out the great *Principia* in the same short period of time.

Newton's mind was overflowing with the results of more

than twenty years of original scientific thinking, and he plunged into the gigantic task of putting it all on paper.

He drove himself so unmercifully that Halley, Wren, and others feared for his health. Yet once having undertaken the job, it was like Newton to see it through to the end—whatever might happen to himself. Proofs, theorems, propositions, equations, principles, precisely-labeled diagrams—these were what Newton lived and breathed during the rest of 1685 and the year 1686.

Luckily some details of Newton's personal life during the writing of the *Principia* are known. Sometime in 1683 Newton hired a young assistant named Humphrey Newton to be his *amanuensis,* or secretary. Humphrey was no relation to Isaac Newton, although strangely enough he came from Newton's old school village of Grantham.

It was Humphrey Newton who copied out the original manuscript of the *Principia* for the printer from Newton's own jumble of notes. The young secretary later sketched several word-pictures of the genius at work on his great book.

Humphrey Newton recalls that he never saw Isaac Newton laugh. The secretary also wrote that his master was "very meek, sedate and humble, never seemingly angry, of profound thought, his countenance mild, and pleasant . . ." Newton also appears to have taken very little exercise or recreation, devoting all his time to his work.

"He ate very sparingly," recalls Humphrey Newton again, "nay, ofttimes he forgot to eat at all, so that, going into his chambers, I have found his mess untouched. . . .

He very rarely went to bed till two or three of the clock, sometimes not till five or six . . ."

Humphrey Newton also recalls that when he reminded

At work on the Principia. *Newton's young secretary recalls that he never saw the great philosopher laugh.*

the Lucasian Professor that he had neglected to eat, Newton would mumble a surprised, "Have I?" Then he would shuffle to the table and, still standing, absent-mindedly peck at a bit of food. "For," run Humphrey's notes, "I cannot say that I ever saw him sit at a table by himself."

Neither did the secretary see Newton take wine, ale, or beer in anything but moderation. "He very rarely went to dine in the hall, except on some public days, and then if he had not been minded, would go very carelessly, with shoes down at the heel, stockings untied . . . and his head scarcely combed."

From these recollections, we get a picture of a man entirely devoted to his work, pacing his study, hardly aware of what was happening around him—and not caring. Newton also walked in his garden a great deal, but might at any moment stop and rush upstairs to jot down some thoughts—without even bothering to sit down!

And yet, while he was writing the *Principia*, Newton did have one great relaxation—alchemy—of which one of the chief concerns was the changing of other metals to gold. His laboratory was set up in a corner of the garden near the Trinity College gate.

In order to carry out his beloved experiments Newton needed furnaces, and these he built himself with homemade bricks. Newton's secretary also recalls that at this time he spent "about six weeks in his laboratory, the fire scarce going out either night or day, he sitting up one night and I another, until he had finished his chemical experiments."

Newton's great interest in alchemy, together with the long, painstaking notes he left, have caused many scholars to wonder whether, in some unexplained way, he suspected that the very nature of the universe lay locked away in the chemicals with which he was experimenting.

Surely it was not gold alone that Newton sought to produce from the more ordinary metals. Did Newton, in fact, suspect that tremendous energy might be released by such changes—what today would be called nuclear energy?

That he might well have suspected something like this appears in another part of his young secretary's writings: "What his aim might be I was not able to penetrate into, but his pains, his diligence at these . . . times made me think that he aimed at something beyond the reach of human art and industry."

Meanwhile Newton had set out to accomplish a tremendous task. Many scientific problems had to be stated clearly as well as answered exactly. Pacing his room night after night, Newton knew that he must deal squarely with five questions.

Specifically, this is what he must do.

(1) He must state that if there is no force acting on a moving body, then that body will continue to move in one direction only, at one constant speed; and further, if there is any change of speed or direction, that change is in proportion to the force or combination of forces that causes it.

(2) He must clearly define the kind of force that explains the motion of the planets, and he must prove the mathematical law on which it is based.

(3) He must prove that gravitation really exists, and show especially how it affects the moon's motion around the earth.

(4) He must satisfactorily link to some of Kepler's previous mathematics the law of gravitation as it applies

[103]

to the planetary motions. For this alone, he must show strong mathematical proof.

(5) He must somehow fit the entire solar system into

Newton, the alchemist, at work in his garden laboratory.

the greater picture of *universal* gravitation. And he must explain the motions of the comets and satellites, as well as the mighty motions of the tides.

In undertaking this great task Newton did not have to depend on the observations of earlier astronomers. Several years before, he had exchanged letters concerning the motions of comets with the brilliant astronomer, John Flamsteed.

King Charles II had appointed Flamsteed a Court astronomer at the early age of twenty-nine. Later, when the famed Greenwich Observatory was built, Flamsteed was named Astronomer Royal. Although the two men quarreled in later years, it was still Flamsteed who furnished Newton with the latest information about Saturn's orbit, the moons of Jupiter and Saturn, and the tides.

In writing the *Principia*, Newton saw that it logically was not one book at all, but three. Book I of the work was soon ready, for it was actually an expansion of Newton's earlier paper, *De Motu*. By the middle of the year 1685, Book II was ready. Book III, however, was a much more difficult task because in it Newton had to take observed planetary motions and other astronomical data, such as those provided by Flamsteed, and fit them into his theory.

Finally in April of the following year, Edmund Halley announced before the Royal Society that "Mr. Newton has an incomparable Treatise of Motion almost ready for the press." Actually, when the manuscript was first presented to the Society, it consisted only of Book I. But the vast importance of the whole work was immediately recognized and Halley was asked to investigate the details of having it printed—not, however, as a mere entry in the Society's *Transactions*, but as a real book.

At the next meeting of the Royal Society in May, it was resolved that "Mr. Newton's work should be printed forthwith." Unfortunately, when the Society took stock of their finances, it was discovered that there was not nearly enough money left to pay for the printing of Newton's work; the year before, the Society's available funds had been nearly exhausted in printing a book on fishes.

Another month went by and nothing was done. Here indeed was another historical curiosity in Newton's life. A swiftly outdated book concerning marine life—of which nearly nothing valuable was known in Newton's time— was being seen through the press at great expense, while the manuscript of the great *Principia*—containing basic laws of the universe as true then as they are today—lay gathering dust!

The generous Halley, however, could not bear to see his friend's brilliant work go unpublished. He talked with the members of the Society and soon that body adopted a most remarkable resolution concerning Newton's manuscript: "That Mr. Halley undertake the business of looking after it, and printing it at his own charge, which he engaged to do"!

Halley was determined that his friend's work should see the light of day—cost him what it might. The young astronomer's willingness to pay for the printing was all the more remarkable because he did not have much money. Although he was later to win fame himself, together with the high post of Astronomer Royal, he was far from being wealthy in 1685; further, he had a wife and family to provide for. Yet if Halley had done nothing more than make possible the publication of the *Principia* he would have won great fame.

Meanwhile, as Newton was deep in the preparation of

Book III, Robert Hooke again entered the picture. It can be easily imagined what the cranky, ailing scientist's feelings were concerning Newton's discoveries. Here were the very principles and proofs for which he himself had yearned, now snatched from him by a younger man.

While Hooke had been idly speculating in his mysterious way, Newton, by sheer hard work, had brilliantly answered many of the problems of the universe. Although Hooke could hardly deny the greatness of Newton's mathematical proof of the law of gravitation, he began muttering to certain members of the Royal Society that he—Hooke himself—had first suggested parts of the law to Newton!

Actually, of course, the basic idea had occurred to several people independently. As we know, Newton had discovered it as early as 1666 at Woolsthorpe. Later, even Halley and Wren had separately managed to arrive at it from one of Kepler's laws. Others on the Continent, notably Huygens, had also worked it out independently.

Fearing that Hooke's jealous claims would certainly upset Newton, Halley discussed the matter with Francis Aston, another of Newton's friends and the newly-elected Secretary of the Royal Society.

Knowing that Newton hated bickering of this kind, they at first decided not to tell him of Hooke's claims. But Halley, realizing that the Lucasian Professor would hear of the Hooke matter in time anyway, decided that the wisest course would be to write Newton a tactful letter.

While Halley broke the news as gently as he could, Newton was still very angry. Extremely sensitive in such matters, he was not so much pained about who had been first to discover the law as he was at the hint that he had stolen it from Hooke.

Reviewing the whole history of how he had come upon his law, and quoting from old letters that proved it, Newton replied point by point to Hooke's claims, as he had before.

Halley did all he could to prevent further scandal, suggesting that all Hooke really wanted was credit for helping give Newton a first hint of parts of the law. Halley further suggested it might be proper that the author of the *Principia* "make some mention of him in the preface."

This made Newton even more angry. Not only did he bitterly attack Hooke, but he wrote a furious letter to Halley saying that, far from giving credit to Hooke in the preface of Book III, he meant not to publish that book at all!

Newton's outburst shocked the faithful Halley. This book was to be the high point of Newton's whole work. Moreover, there were to be contained in it the final great astronomical ideas that were of special interest to Halley— mathematical proofs that applied to planetary motions, lunar theory, the theories of comets and tides.

Fortunately, Halley, with his usual tact, succeeded in calming down the author of the *Principia*. Work went ahead as planned on Book III—*De Mundi Systemate,* or "System of the World." In the end, Newton regretted his bitter reply to Hooke and finally stated in the book that certain mathematics had been worked out from Kepler's work by himself, and separately by Wren, Hooke, and Halley.

Early in July of 1686, the *imprimatur,* or license to print the book in the name of the Royal Society, was given by the current President—none other than the famous diarist, Samuel Pepys.

Within a few weeks the actual printing of Book I began. In March, 1687, Book II reached the Royal Society, and a month later, the famous Book III.

It is indeed surprising that it took Newton only eighteen months to produce this famous work, for the trouble with Robert Hooke was not his only interruption.

King Charles II had died some months before and now the narrow-minded, obstinate James II had taken his brother's place on the throne. James was a staunch believer in an absolute monarchy, and he happened to be a Roman Catholic who was determined to force his own religion on the entire English people.

The stubborn threat on the part of the new King naturally alarmed all peace-loving Englishmen, whether Protestant or Catholic, since the country had been mostly of the Protestant faith for centuries. If the King were to carry out his wishes by force, there was sure to be trouble.

Blindly, James decided to force his will on the people. A good place to begin, he reasoned, was at the universities, which had been strongholds of Protestantism for many years. The first blow was struck at the University of Oxford, where James forced the officials to install a Catholic of the King's choosing to a high University post. Of course, the more such powerful officials James could place there, the quicker he could force his own faith on the rest.

The King struck next at Newton's own Cambridge in February of 1687. James sent off a royal command to the University authorities demanding that a Benedictine monk, Father Alban Francis, be admitted to the Master of Arts degree. This was clearly a threat to University government since the holder of a master's degree could vote in that institution's Senate. If the King succeeded in installing one of his people, others would quickly follow.

The vice-chancellor of the University, Dr. John Pechell, politely refused to carry out the royal order. Unless Father Francis agreed to take the usual oaths of allegiance to the University, it was not in Pechell's power to grant him the Master of Arts degree.

James was furious at this defiance of his will, and he quickly ordered the Vice-chancellor to appear before the High Commission Court at Westminster, accompanied by eight representatives of the University Senate. Newton was one of these eight. He determined to stick firmly by the University's cause and not to give in to the king's wishes.

Presiding over this court was the cruel and vicious Royal Judge, Lord Jeffreys, a man who was feared and hated throughout England. The Vice-chancellor of Cambridge was a scholarly and timid man, and he was soon frightened speechless by Lord Jeffreys' rough accusations. The other deputies stood helplessly by, forbidden to say anything in defense of the University's position.

Although Vice-chancellor Pechell was stripped of his post, the champions of the University eventually won out.

It was Newton who pointed out the technicality that defeated James II and his royal lackey, Lord Jeffreys. Rant and rave as the latter would, the University had a good legal case.

Newton had quietly informed his colleagues beforehand that the only type of degrees that could be granted without taking the usual oaths of allegiance were *honorary* ones: men who held such degrees were permitted no voice or vote in the University's governing body! And, since Father Francis would not take the oaths, any degree he received was necessarily honorary.

Lord Jeffreys was furious and ordered the Cambridge representatives out of court with a last parting insult. "As for you," he snarled at them, "most of you are divines. I will therefore send you home with a text of Scripture, 'Go your way and sin no more, lest a worst thing happen to you.' "

Isaac Newton, himself not a "divine" for he had never taken holy orders, had to take this insult without replying —a man who was just putting the finishing touches on a book that would outlive dozens of royal bullies like King James and Lord Jeffreys.

Newton and his colleagues returned to Cambridge victorious. In his rooms between the Great Gate and Trinity Chapel, Newton found a mountain of printer's proofs to be read and corrected.

Within two months after the Lucasian Professor had been rudely ordered out of the royal court, the *Principia* was published—dedicated to the Royal Society "flourishing under his august Majesty James II"!

◆

FOURTEEN

The *Principia*

━━━━━━━━━━◆◆◆━━━━━━━━━━

N EWTON'S crowning achievement, the *Principia*, is a book that is little read today. Ask for it in the average bookstore and it will not be available. Many public libraries do not have a copy on their shelves, either in its original Latin or in the English translation.

Today, the best place to find the *Principia* is in a rare bookshop or the reference room of a large library. It is worth a trip to either to see the precise, majestic way in which Isaac Newton set down and proved his great theories.

It is true that this book, as Newton wrote it, is hard to find. But throughout the world there are still thousands of shelves containing tens of thousands of books, in every one of which is printed modernized versions of the basic truths in the *Principia*. Since Newton's day, language and methods of presenting knowledge have changed—but the same truths, however printed or expressed in modern textbooks, remain fundamentally the same.

The *Principia* is not merely a collection of knowledge of the past with mere traces of originality here and there. On the contrary, it is one of the most original books ever written by one author.

Not only did Newton set down for the first time the

basic laws of mechanics, but he himself invented the mathematical machinery needed to prove them. Never before had there been a statement of the laws of motion that bear Newton's name today. Brilliant answers to problems that had occupied the best minds for centuries are presented in the *Principia*. And throughout all its pages this astonishing book has an air of dignity and simplicity, of quiet grandeur that raises the work and its author to an unequaled level of scientific achievement.

The original *Principia* was published in July of 1687. It was a rather small-sized book containing about five hundred pages and illustrated with many diagrams in the form of woodcuts. Bound in calfskin, it sold for nine shillings.

Halley, who had patiently acted as Newton's editor, was immensely pleased with the result. Again showing his unfailing generosity, he wrote to Newton on publication: "I have at length brought your book to an end, and I hope it will please you. . . . I will present from you the book . . . to the Royal Society, Mr. Boyle, Mr. Paget, Mr. Flamsteed, and if there be any else in town that you design to gratify that way."

As a matter of fact, Halley probably got his investment back in a short time, for the *Principia* sold quickly. When copies of the first printing became scarce, many people were soon paying three and four times the original cost. There is even a case on record of a Scotsman who, unable to secure a copy at a reasonable price, copied out the whole book by hand.

Of the many things that Newton accomplished in the

PHILOSOPHIÆ
NATURALIS
PRINCIPIA
MATHEMATICA

Autore *IS. NEWTON*, *Trin. Coll. Cantab. Soc.* Matheseos
Professore *Lucasiano*, & Societatis Regalis Sodali.

IMPRIMATUR
S. PEPYS, *Reg. Soc.* PRÆSES.
Julii 5. 1686.

LONDINI,

Jussu *Societatis Regiæ* ac Typis *Josephi Streater.* Prostat apud
plures Bibliopolas. *Anno* MDCLXXXVII.

Title page of the first edition of the Principia. *Note the name
of the famous diarist, Samuel Pepys, who, as President of the
Royal Society, gave the* imprimatur, *or license to print the book.*

Principia, some of the major ones can be briefly touched upon here. Newton begins his work immediately and on a sweeping scale by setting down, in the introduction, his famous Laws of Motion.

Newton's laws are these:

FIRST LAW: *A body at rest will remain at rest and a body in motion will continue in motion at a constant speed in a straight line unless acted upon by some outside force.*

The First Law introduces the idea of *inertia* (from the Latin word meaning "idleness"). Suppose that you are riding on a bus going 20 miles an hour. The bus stops suddenly; it is no longer going 20 miles an hour. But you are. Unless you grab a strap or a handrail, you will keep right on going since you are a "body" in motion.

This forward thrust that you have experienced is a demonstration of *inertia,* which is simply a one-word description of an object's tendency to remain in its condition of rest or motion. And the amount of inertia an object has is in proportion to the amount of force needed to slow it down, speed it up, stop it, or change its direction.

Again, suppose you started a toy railroad car rolling along a smooth, hard track. According to Newton's First Law, the car should keep moving along the track at one constant speed. It doesn't, of course, because the Law says nothing about friction. If left to itself, the car will eventually slow up and stop because the wheels encounter the friction of the track and the body of the car meets the friction of the air through which it must move. The greater the friction, the sooner the car will stop. The smaller the friction, the longer the car will keep traveling. Of course, if all friction could be eliminated, the *inertia* of the car would keep it moving indefinitely at one constant speed.

On the earth's surface, it is difficult to demonstrate the First Law of Motion because air-resistance (drag or friction), and the tremendous forces of gravity, prevent an object from traveling at one constant speed in a straight line. But one of the best proofs of the First Law is found in the movements of the heavenly bodies, which meet practically no friction in their travels through space. The only strong forces acting on the planets, for example, are the gravitational forces that hold them in their orbits. The planets are truly bodies in motion. They have been going at about the same rate ever since man first observed them. These bodies give ample proof that an object would indeed move in a straight line were it not acted on by outside forces.

Modern artificial satellites, such as the Sputniks, Explorers, and Discoverers also obey Newton's First Law in the same way; many of these, however, have not been given orbits completely free of the earth's atmosphere and as a result have burned up due to air friction. But space ships of the future will most certainly be able to prove Newton's First Law in actual practice. In free space, clear of any noticeable gravitational forces, the captain of such a ship need only "gun" his rockets once, then switch them off. Whatever speed he has attained, he will keep going at in a straight line—forever—unless of course he enters the gravitational field of another heavenly body.

SECOND LAW: *Any change in motion of a body is in proportion to the force pressing on it, and takes place in the*

*direction of the straight line in which the pressing force
acts.*

In stating his Second Law, Newton was giving scientists
in his own time as well as today, a valuable tool by which
forces can be measured. By measuring the mass (weight,
for all practical purposes) that a given force moves, and
any change in speed that such a force brings about, we
have a trustworthy method of measuring the *magnitude,*
or size, of that force. The mathematical relationships provided by the Second Law also allow scientists to measure
the force of gravity at any point on the earth's surface—
at the equator, the north pole or wherever. The ability to
make such calculations is of great value to scientists in
planning the orbit of an artificial satellite, or man-made
moon.

THIRD LAW: *For every action exerted on a body, there
is an equal and opposite reaction.*

Another way of stating the Third Law is this: *whenever
one body exerts a force on another, the second body exerts
an equal and opposite force on the first body.*

The Third Law of Motion is perhaps most fascinating
of all. Newton himself pointed out that when you press
a stone with your finger, your finger is also pressed back
by the stone. Similarly, when you stand on the floor, the
weight of your body pushes down on the floor; but, at the
same time, the floor pushes back up on your feet with
exactly the same force. If you kick a football, it will react
with equal force against your foot. When you fire a rifle,
the forward thrust of the bullet is matched by a backward
thrust or "kick" against your shoulder.

Nowhere else today, perhaps, is Newton's Third Law of Motion of such great importance as in the field of jet and rocket flight.

In the case of jet-propelled planes, the backward thrust of gases issuing from the jet engine reacts against the engine itself and causes a forward thrust. It is *not* true that the rearward gases push against the air; if it were, Newton's Third Law would not be true. But jet engines are air-breathers and the hot gases burned in them feed on the air supply they take from the atmosphere.

Rockets, on the other hand, carry their fuel along with them and can travel in outer space where there is no air and, hence, no air-resistance. In the near-perfect vacuum of space, Newton's Third Law operates ideally. The powerful thrust inside a rocket's engine results in an equal and opposite thrust forward of the rocket itself because there is no air-drag in outer space. Hence, fantastic speeds of thousands of miles an hour are possible. In the future, when man will have developed his rocket engines to the point where he can reach other planets of the solar system, he will have done so in accordance with Newton's all-important Third Law of Motion.

Both in the world of science and in our own daily lives, Newton's three brief statements about motion have the most gigantic meaning. They are always and everywhere true. At every point, they underlie the methods by which today's physicists and astronomers search for new knowledge.

The principles that Isaac Newton set forth in the *Principia,* it is true, were not all discovered only by him.

Newton well knew that he had inherited much from earlier scientists and even those of his own time. Kepler had already suggested some of the mathematics he used. Galileo had furnished invaluable data upon which Newton had based the first two laws of motion. There were also hints of the third law in the work of Huygens, Wren, and Wallis. Yet it was Newton who was able to see farther into these isolated theories and combine them into a single, vast system with mathematical proof.

The main work of the *Principia* is in the first two books of the *De Motu Corporum,* or "The Motion of Bodies," and in a third book, *De Mundi Systemate,* or "System of the World."

Book I begins with a brief account of his method of fluxions, which is the first printed statement of his discovery aside from brief papers about twenty years before. Apparently Newton had read a paper or two of Leibnitz' work on the subject and felt that the time had come to give his own fluxion theory to the world.

Newton then turned to the motion of an object that is under an attraction to some fixed point, such as a satellite orbiting its planet, or a planet's motion around the sun. When this orbit is in the form of an ellipse, the force must bear a certain relation to the distance. Here again, Newton employed the inverse square law, particularly where a center of gravitational attraction was at one focus of an elliptical orbit. Newton was thus able to show how it is possible to describe a planet's position at any time in its orbit.

It had also become clear to Newton that every heavenly

body attracted every other heavenly body. The sun attracts and is attracted by the planets. The earth attracts and is attracted by the moon. But, wrote Newton, the sun is so large in comparison to even the largest of the solar system's planets that in describing any one planet's motion it is permissible to neglect any other attraction on it except the sun's. In turn, the same would apply to the satellites. The moon, for example, is so close to the earth about which it revolves that the sun's pull on it could largely be neglected.

But what about a *really exact* description of the moon's motion? This was a problem that Newton had worried about for years. More than once Newton said that "his head never ached but when he was studying the lunar theory."

When he wrote of this problem in the *Principia* he saw that Kepler's laws must not be *wholly* correct—only nearly so. For Kepler had lived at a time when it was not possible to measure the *perturbations,* or small changes, in the motions of the planets. Although Kepler's laws of planetary motions *did* give a very accurate description of a planet's motion for a few revolutions, scientists in Newton's time knew that these could add up to serious errors in their calculations. The moon's changes in motion, for example, were very large and had been noticed as early as 400 B.C.

Even today, mathematicians and astronomers have not been able to fully solve the problem of *perturbations.* It is very much to Newton's credit that he made such progress in explaining them. He showed that the attractive

force of the sun would explain some of the known perturbations of the moon, and actually figured out some of
those changes correctly. And, he was able to predict others
that were found to be right long after his death!

Newton went on to state what is perhaps the very
cornerstone of the theory of gravitation: *Every particle of
matter in the universe exerts a pull upon every other particle of matter.*

Practically, this meant that if the matter in any spherical body, say a planet, is arranged symmetrically about
its center, there is the same gravitational force at any point
on its surface as there would be if all the matter were
concentrated at the center. Here, Newton knew that he
had the key to many mysteries, among them the explanation of the oceans' tides.

Book II of the *Principia* deals with a body's motion
through mediums offering resistance to such motion. Newton said that this resistance—for example that of the air—
is always proportional to the speed of the body. Thus
Newton, living some three hundred years before com-
mercial air flight, foresaw one of the very problems with
which modern aeronautical engineers constantly have to
deal; namely, the streamlining of their aircraft.

Other sections of the *Principia* go on to discuss theories
of pendulums, wave motion in fluids, and theories of
light. Newton also wrote of wave motion as it applies to
the traveling of sound waves through the air. Today any
visitor to Cambridge University can test the famous four-
fold echo with which Newton himself experimented in
Neville's Court at Trinity.

Then, in the great Book III—the very book which he threatened not to publish because of Robert Hooke—Newton united all the various phenomena of the solar system by means of his universal law of gravitation.

In brilliant proof after brilliant proof, Newton established the gravitation of Jupiter, Saturn, the sun, and the earth. He also provided proof of his own inverse square law.

Finally, he stated the great law of universal gravitation on which his fame rests; namely, that all bodies attract each other with a force proportional to the product of their masses, and inversely proportional to the square of the distance between them.

Newton further showed that since the planets hurtling through space met very little resistance, their motion could be expected to go on forever. Moreover, each planet revolved around the sun in an elliptical orbit, which has a focus at the sun.

All the heavenly bodies, wrote Newton, must obey this universal law. Thus, two heavenly bodies mutually attracting each other would have similar orbits about a common center of gravity and also about each other. If three such heavenly bodies attract each other—such as the earth, the sun, and the moon—then there will be certain small changes in their orbits. Hence, the motion of the moon is irregular, or *perturbed,* because it attracts (and is attracted by) the sun at the same time that it attracts (and is attracted by) the earth.

Today we know that when Newton called his law of gravitation *universal,* he meant just that. This attraction or pull applies to every object *everywhere,* no matter where it is located. Not only does it apply to the heavenly bodies; it explains why a baseball drops to the ground from your hand, why a length of garden hose sags when it is tied between two trees, why even such tiny particles as dust eventually settle on a bookshelf.

Newton then ended the *Principia* with a section on comets. Though these mysterious heavenly visitors were formerly regarded as unexplainable, Newton said that the comets, too, obeyed the law of universal gravitation. Here again the author was breaking new ground, for he stated— and rightly—that these were bodies moving under the attraction of the sun in very long elliptical orbits.

This, then, was Newton's great work. The knowledge contained in it had been written down in eighteen months. Yet over and over again, the greatest triumphs of human thought have been traced directly back to this remarkable book.

The later work of such men as Laplace and Lagrange and their successors was based upon Newton's findings. So was the discovery in 1846 of the planet Neptune, whose orbit was worked out before it was actually sighted. Today, scientists can calculate an artificial satellite's orbit, accurate to within seconds, because of Newton's work.

And what stands today as the most outstanding scientific achievement of our time—Albert Einstein's *Theory of Relativity*—is also built solidly on Newton's discoveries. Indeed, the very fact that gravitation *is* universal forms the chief argument for the Theory of Relativity.

FIFTEEN

Halley's Comet

No one had waited more eagerly for the publication of the *Principia* than Newton's admirer, Edmund Halley. Halley was a jovial, fun-loving man in leisure hours, but a hard-working, dedicated astronomer in the observatory. Halley read Newton's Book III on comets with great interest, his head full of many unanswered questions.

The centuries-old mystery of the sudden appearance and disappearance of comets had puzzled Halley for years. Long objects of dread and superstition, these strange heavenly visitors glided into the solar system, made directly for the sun, hovered there for a short period, and then were as mysteriously hurled away again. Never did they seem to return—once observed, the comets were apparently lost forever; they seemed to obey no law of motion whatsoever.

And yet, as Halley read on in the *Principia,* he realized that Newton was saying just the opposite thing. Comets *did* return to the neighborhood of the sun! Their motion was not "lawless" at all, but must obey the law of universal gravitation, just as the planets did.

Halley became greatly excited. Newton had offered no

actual proof of the comet's return. Could he—Halley—
come to Newton's aid?

Halley thought back to the great comet that had
appeared in the sky in the year 1682. He himself had
observed it carefully and calculated its path when it
approached the sun. As usual, its luminous tail, many
thousands of miles long, always pointed away from the
sun while its great head pointed toward it. But the sun
had seemed to hurl it away at such a wide angle that
Halley did not see how it could possibly return. To
Halley, the great comet's orbit appeared to be an open
one, not the closed orbit of an ellipse.

Yet here was Newton demonstrating in the *Principia*
that very long elliptic orbits with one focus at the sun
were indeed possible. Newton also suggested that comets,
because they moved in these long ellipses, could be predicted to return in a certain period of time!

Halley was both amazed and puzzled. A comet became
visible to those on earth only when it was near the sun.
Also, the sun seemed to make the comet throw off matter
from its head in the form of a tail. Thus the comet remained invisible much of the time, except for a very
short interval when it was near the sun.

Furthermore, thought Halley, when the comet shot off
into space again, how could it possibly be traced all
around its immense elliptical orbit to prove Newton right?

Halley became fascinated with the possibility that
comets returned, and he became interested especially in
the great 1682 comet. He discussed the matter with
Newton. The author of the *Principia* insisted that the

comet had probably been in the sun's neighborhood before, and would be observed again. But one thing was
obvious to both men: the comet might take as long as a
hundred years to return. Neither man would be alive
when it came back into view.

An idea struck Halley. True, they would have to rely
on some future astronomer to verify the comet's return,
but what would prevent him—Halley—from searching
about in old records to find out whether the visitor had
been sighted *in the past?*

Halley proposed this idea to Newton. The older man
nodded and indicated that though it would be a tremendous amount of work, it was certainly worth undertaking.

Halley therefore set about examining all reliable observations of comets that had appeared in the past. The task
was all the more difficult since the accuracy of such descrip-
tions must not depend on mere mentions alone, but on
reliable sightings from at least *three positions* to correctly
determine the comet's position. Newton himself had suggested this proof in the *Principia.*

Edmund Halley spent much of the next twenty years
of his life poring over ancient books and manuscripts,
searching for sufficient proof to verify the comet's previous
visits to the solar system. Years passed, the old records
revealed nothing, yet Halley did not give up the search.

Finally his efforts were rewarded. Halley discovered that
in the year 1607 Kepler himself had observed a comet
answering the description of the one in 1682. Exactly
75 years had gone by between the two sightings. But had

Edmund Halley became fascinated with the possibility that comets returned to the solar system.

[127]

it been the same comet in both cases? Halley, bursting with excitement, felt sure that it was.

And yet, as Newton pointed out, it may only have been an interesting coincidence. He urged Halley to continue his search back through the centuries. The job, after all, would be easier now for, if Newton's theory were correct, a record of the comet should exist somewhere 75 *years before* 1607.

Halley once again took up the task of reading through old records—but these of course were much older and less accurate. Yet Halley kept at it.

Again years went by. Then Halley succeeded in tracking down another reference to a comet—nearly identical to the one of 1682—in 1531! Although the interval this time was 76 years instead of 75, Halley was not worried. It was perfectly possible that the comet had been slowed down by some planetary perturbance.

With this much evidence, other astronomers might have been convinced that these sightings were all of one and the same comet, but not Edmund Halley. Once again, he took up the search through older and older records. Then, in an ancient manuscript, he happened across the mention of a comet sighted in 1456—another 75-year interval!

Halley himself was finally convinced. The evidence seemed sure. In the year 1705, he announced publicly that the comet he had observed in 1682 would reappear. It would, he predicted, come again about the end of 1758 or the beginning of 1759, its period taking a bit longer due to a severe perturbation by a near approach to Jupiter.

Halley had looked back through hundreds of years for

proof of cometary return; now, with Newton's aid, he looked into the future. Halley and Newton grew older; then Newton, who died in 1727, was no longer there to watch. Halley continued his vigil alone, imagining his comet speeding on its long and lonely way, past the orbit of earth, the planets, deeper and deeper into space.

Knowing that he could not live to see the year of the comet's return, Halley died in the hope that, if it did come back as predicted, posterity "would acknowledge that this was first discovered by an Englishman."

Then, on Christmas of 1758, sixteen years after Halley's death, a brilliant white light glided into the evening sky. Newton's old friend had been correct! Astronomers the world over immediately named it "Halley's Comet."

Years later, in 1835, the comet was seen again—and again in 1910. Even now Halley's Comet is wending on its long cigar-shaped elliptical path through space and is expected to reappear in the year 1986.

The world indeed will never forget Edmund Halley's nationality, nor that his memory was thus linked with the man he admired with such devotion.

—◆—

SIXTEEN

Guardian of the
Coinage

————◆·◆————

SHORTLY after the *Principia's* publication, Edmund Halley noticed how tired Newton seemed. The astronomer thought Newton should take a rest from scientific work, and urged him many times to do so. Finally, Newton took Halley's advice.

The Cambridge authorities, remembering Newton's service to them in the Lord Jeffreys matter, elected him a Member of Parliament for the University. Newton was a loyal supporter of the new king, William of Orange. A Whig in politics, Newton was also a strong believer in religious freedom and a stout opponent of all forms of oppression.

Thus the great scientist took up a new life in London— a life which, after his long years of quiet study at Cambridge, he found immensely stimulating. And yet, being in the London whirl also caused Newton to reflect more and more on his own position. He was now nearly fifty years old, and he had spent almost all of his mature years in scientific inquiry. Although he was recognized as a great scientist, his fame had brought him little money. Compared to others, he was still a relatively poor university professor. The needs of his relatives and dependents were an increasing drain on his finances.

For the first time in his life, Newton was giving some serious thought to his future security.

After more than a year of service in the Convention Parliament, during which he gained important support for the new king at the University, Newton made his wants known.

His influential friends, among them the philosopher John Locke and the diarist Samuel Pepys, tried to secure for him some public post worthy of his greatness.

One prominent young man, Charles Montagu, a fellow Member of Parliament, and later to become the powerful Lord Halifax, did all he could to aid Newton. But despite all his friends' efforts, the men to whom they applied seemed too busy to bother about a mathematician whose work they could not understand. Post after post fell vacant, but Newton, for one reason or another, was always brushed aside in favor of another man.

Discouraged, the author of the *Principia* returned to his lonely life of study at Cambridge. Other things, too, had happened to make Newton gloomy. His mother had fallen seriously ill. He sat up whole nights with her, doing everything in his power to lighten her sufferings. Soon, in spite of all his efforts, Hannah Smith died, without seeing her son Isaac given the honors that he so deserved from England.

Toward the end of 1692, the strain that he had been under began to tell. Despite his general good health,

Newton suffered a slight nervous breakdown. He began to brood for long hours about his failure to obtain a governmental post. Now his years of insufficient sleep and irregular eating habits began to catch up with him. He was often physically unwell and grew more and more irritable, flying into a rage over the smallest matter. More than anything else, he resented the fact that he must go hat-in-hand to influential men for a job, almost like a beggar!

Worn out by the terrific strain of writing the *Principia,* unhappy and bitter, Newton came to believe that he had been deserted by the very friends who loved him most. In this bitter mood, he sent off angry letters to Samuel Pepys, John Locke, Halley, and others, charging them all with being disloyal to him.

Puzzled and hurt, Newton's friends feared for the great scientist's health. They banded together to see what could be done about Newton. Not only would they try harder to get him a post of honor but they would send someone to find out what was worrying him.

Their choice fell on John Millington, a personable young scholar at Cambridge's Magdalene College. Millington paid Newton a visit, sending back word that while the author of the *Principia* had suffered some nervous attacks, he seemed on the road to recovery. Also, Newton sincerely regretted the angry letters he had written while under his nervous strain.

After a few months, the Lucasian Professor was completely himself once more. He plunged into creative scientific work again, collecting additional data from

Flamsteed for his theory of lunar motion and preparing additions and corrections for the *Principia's* second edi-

Breakdown. Worn out from writing the Principia, *unhappy and bitter, Newton came to believe that his best friends had deserted him.*

tion. Newton was also busy again with his beloved chemical experiments.

Little did he realize that his lifelong interest in metals and alloys was soon to be put to practical use. For a complete change in his life and work was in the making. His friends were seeing to that.

Good news came at last from the fast-rising politician, Charles Montagu. An intimate friend of Newton's, Montagu had been appointed Chancellor of the Exchequer in 1694. More than once, Montagu had discussed the serious state of English coinage with Newton and others. Both gold and silver were legal tender in the land, but the silver coins had lost value because they were made of cheap and inferior alloys. Also, for decades, people had been in the habit of "clipping coins"; that is, slicing off bits of silver from their unmilled edges and then passing the mutilated coins off at their original value.

Montagu realized that things were in a very bad state indeed. English silver was even being refused by the Bank of Amsterdam, then the financial center of Europe. He was now in a position to do something about it, and he determined to restore the coinage to its full value. In Newton, Montagu realized he had the perfect man for carrying through the difficult task.

The Wardenship of the Royal Mint had become vacant early in 1696, and in March of that year Montagu wrote to Newton saying that the King had appointed him to the post. Newton accepted and took over his new duties as Warden of the Mint in London without delay.

Former Wardens of the Mint had looked on the position as one that required little work but offered high pay. But Newton took his job very seriously. Much work was necessary in the substituting of new coins for the old ones, for all the former coins had to be called in and new ones issued by a certain date.

Finally in 1699 Newton had successfully completed the entire task of recoining, for which a grateful king and nation thanked him. In that same year, he was appointed Master of the Mint, a high post that paid about 1500 pounds yearly and which Newton was to hold for the rest of his life.

By now, Newton had become a permanent resident of London. He had taken a house in Jermyn Street near Piccadilly Square, and with him he had taken as housekeeper the daughter born to his mother by a third marriage. This young woman, Catharine Barton, was vivacious and lively, and brightened Newton's later years considerably. For now Newton had a great deal of entertaining to do and a beautiful and accomplished young lady, noted for her conversation and wit, was a great asset to him.

From 1665 to 1696—just about half of his adult years— Newton had been a scientist, and had worked hard to discover scientific laws. He had thirty-one more years to live, and these he spent in the service of his nation and as the undisputed leader of British science.

Living in London as he did, Newton decided in 1699 to give up his old post as Lucasian Professor in favor of another man, William Whiston. But he still served Cambridge by once more being elected to Parliament in 1701; there he continued until the death of King William III and the succession of Queen Anne to the throne.

There were some persons who regarded Newton's living

in London as a great loss to British science. Others even claimed that the great philosopher had lost his abilities. But Newton was far from exhausted scientifically. The

Newton as Warden of the Royal Mint, working on the recoinage problem.

truth was that the discoveries he had already made were so great that he could only hope to improve here and there on them in the years that remained.

The greatest minds of the day continually asked Newton's advice on scientific problems and he always gave freely of his time to them. He continued his work on lunar theory and even worked out plans for the first practical sextant, an instrument for navigation on the high seas.

Unfortunately, Newton's later life was made unpleasant by two violent quarrels that dragged on for years. One was with the Astronomer Royal, John Flamsteed, and the other with the German mathematician, Gottfried von Leibnitz.

Newton, in studying the moon's motion, had had to depend heavily on the observations Flamsteed had made. Flamsteed had promised to publish all his findings, but when his progress became slower and slower, Newton complained to the Royal Society. A committee was set up to examine the state of the Royal Observatory, with Newton its chief member. An open quarrel broke out between the two men, which lasted until Flamsteed's death in 1719. To Newton's great satisfaction, however, the deserving Halley was appointed Astronomer Royal the following year.

Even longer and more bitter was the dispute with Leibnitz over who had been the first to invent the calculus. Champions of both men collected evidence on both sides. Angry letters were sent back and forth. Debates raged for years. Finally, the Royal Society appointed a committee to examine all the evidence.

The decision went in favor of Newton, who evidently had used his "fluxions" to solve problems some years before Leibnitz had independently invented his own system. Newton, however, had never bothered to publish his early findings, and it is Leibnitz's superior method of writing down calculus problems that is used everywhere in mathematics today.

Newton being knighted by Queen Anne in 1705 for his great contributions to science.

Meanwhile, the honors that Isaac Newton so richly deserved were beginning to come to him. He was praised by men of science both at home and abroad. In 1699 he had been elected one of the eight foreign members of the French Academy of Sciences.

In November of 1703 he was elected President of the Royal Society itself.

And on April 16, 1705, Queen Anne visited Cambridge and knighted Isaac Newton for his great contributions to English science. This meant that all the rest of his life the dignified title of "Sir" would be added to his name.

Sir Isaac, the unknown country boy from Lincolnshire, had at last won the respect due him from a grateful nation.

SEVENTEEN

Newton's Final Days

Sir Isaac was now a great national and international figure. He lived in fine style, his friends were the highest and most important in the land. He kept a carriage, employed many servants, and entertained hospitably. His salary was more than he needed so that now he could carry on his charitable habits as much as he wished. In particular he was always ready to help young men who showed mathematical ability.

Two of these young men were to repay Sir Isaac handsomely by helping him prepare future editions of the *Principia*. Roger Cotes, a brilliant young mathematician, undertook the great task of preparing the second edition. His death while he was still young was a great blow to Newton, who said, "If Mr. Cotes had lived, we might have known something." And Henry Pemberton, a young physician and mathematician, aided Newton in what was to be the last of his scientific work, the third edition of the *Principia*.

Earlier, in 1704, Newton had allowed his final original work, the *Optics*, to be published. Although it had been ready for years, the author did not wish to have it printed while his old opponent Robert Hooke lived. The book,

Sir Isaac Newton in old age riding in his carriage.

which appeared after Hooke's death in 1703, was an immediate success. Unlike the *Principia,* it appeared in English and in it was contained all of Newton's life's work on the nature of light.

In 1710 Newton moved to a larger house near Leicester Square, a house more suitable for receiving distinguished Englishmen and important foreigners.

Sir Isaac was now nearly seventy, yet he continued to enjoy his remarkable good health. While he was always friendly, he seemed constantly lost in his own thoughts and spoke little in the company of others. Nor had he gotten over his old absent-mindedness. Sometimes he simply sat for long periods in bed, forgetting to dress himself.

There is also the story that Newton was so late in meeting a friend for dinner that the friend, becoming very hungry, ate Newton's food as well as his own. When the great philosopher finally arrived he looked at the empty plates and thought that he had already eaten!

Even when he became eighty, Sir Isaac did not seem greatly aged. Though grown somewhat stout, he was a distinguished-looking man. His hair was now silver-white. He had never had to use spectacles. His mind was alert and lively, and he continued to carry out his duties at the Mint and to preside as President over the Royal Society.

It could not go on. In 1722 he began to suffer the illnesses of old age—first gallstones, followed by inflamed lungs, and then painful attacks of gout in his feet. He traveled less frequently now, for the violent jerking of his carriage through the streets caused him severe pain.

Newton's doctors advised him to move to Kensington where the air was better. Although the change seemed to do him good, he felt he must give up his duties at the Mint. Newton continued to preside at the Royal Society, however, although it is on record that he sometimes fell asleep while sitting in the President's chair.

With the appearance of the third edition of the *Principia,* an amazingly useful and long life was drawing to a close. Sir Isaac himself seemed to know the end was not far off. He studied the history of theology deeply and even prepared a long work on the subject.

Though confined to his house at Kensington, Sir Isaac thought that on February 28, 1727, he felt well enough to make the journey to London to preside at the Royal Society on March 2. He went, but returned on March 4, seriously ill.

It was the beginning of the end. Newton was suffering cruel pains, but he bore them patiently. He even talked cheerfully with those at his bedside. On March 15, he seemed to rally somewhat. But this was an illusion for on March 18 he lapsed into a coma. On March 20, 1727, in the early hours of morning, Newton died painlessly in his sleep.

So ended Newton's life in his eighty-fifth year. The highest possible honors were paid to him. His body lay in state in Westminster Abbey where he was buried on March 28. A monument was erected to his memory. The Mint, where Newton had spent such long hours, issued a medal in his honor.

Rarely had one single man contributed so much to his

own time, as well as to future generations. And rarely had one man done so with such modesty. For Sir Isaac had written these remarkable words to a friend shortly before his death:

> I DO NOT KNOW WHAT I MAY APPEAR TO THE WORLD; BUT TO MYSELF I SEEM TO HAVE BEEN ONLY LIKE A BOY PLAYING ON THE SEASHORE, AND DIVERTING MYSELF NOW AND THEN BY FINDING A SMOOTHER PEBBLE OR A PRETTIER SHELL THAN ORDINARY, WHILST THE GREAT OCEAN OF TRUTH LAY ALL UNDISCOVERED BEFORE ME.

APPENDIX A

CONIC SECTIONS

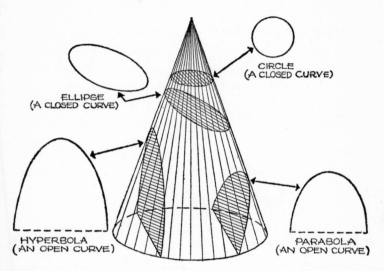

These are the four conic sections—circle, ellipse, hyperbola, and parabola. *They are the curves obtained when a plane surface (like a knife) cuts through a perfect, upright cone. Note that only two of these curves are closed ones—the circle and the ellipse. A body moving in either of these two curves, for example Halley's comet in an ellipse, would ultimately return to the place where it started.*

APPENDIX B

Events in Isaac Newton's Life

Index

DAVID C. KNIGHT is a native of Glens Falls, N.Y. He is a graduate of Union College, Schenectady, N.Y., and attended the Sorbonne in Paris. Currently science editor with a leading New York publishing house, he worked in industrial electronics before entering book publishing. He is the author of *The First Book of Sound* and the forthcoming *The First Book of Air*.